CLANS & TARTANS
OF SCOTLAND

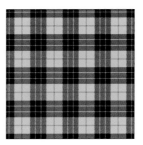

CLANS & TARTANS
OF SCOTLAND

IAIN ZACZEK

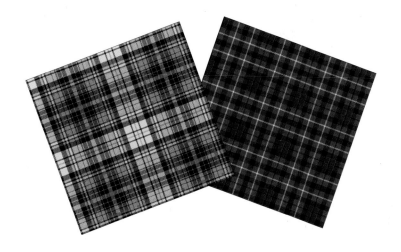

PROSPERO
B·O·O·K·S
A DIVISION OF CHAPTERS INC

FRONT COVER: Caerlaverock Castle
BACK COVER: Castle Stalker
HALF TITLE: MacLeod Dress tartan
TITLE: Eilean Donan castle LEFT: Douglas Ancient tartan
RIGHT: Graham of Montrose tartan

This edition produced for Prospero Books,
a division of Chapters Inc.

First published in Great Britain in 1998 by
Collins & Brown Limited
London House, Great Eastern Wharf
Parkgate Road, London SW11 4NQ

1 3 5 7 9 8 6 4 2

ISBN 1 894102 43 6

Conceived, edited and designed by
Collins & Brown Limited

Editorial Director Colin Ziegler
Art Director Roger Bristow
Editor Claire Waite
Designer Claire Graham
Maps on pages 16 and 17 by Julian Baker

Reproduction by Grafiscan, Italy
Printed and bound in Hong Kong by Dai Nippon

Contents

Introduction

'EVERYONE IS A genealogist!' exclaimed Edward Burt, an 18th-century English lieutenant, as he tried to explain the workings of the clan system to a friend. His amazement was understandable, for the closely-knit structure of the Highland communities could scarcely have been further removed from the centralized governments that existed in most other parts of Europe.

The roots of the system were very ancient, stretching back into Scotland's Celtic past. The country had been occupied by many different peoples – Britons, Romans, Angles, and Vikings – but two races came to dominate. In the north and east, there were the Picts who divided their territories into seven petty kingdoms. In the west, power belonged to the Scots. Originating as an Irish tribe, they migrated from Ulster in the early years of the 6th century AD and founded the settlement of Dalriada in Argyllshire. The kingdoms of the Scots and the Picts were eventually united by Kenneth MacAlpin in c.843.

These peoples were organized along tribal lines. The basic units were the Tuatha ('tribes'), which were banded together into a Mortuath ('great tribe'). These were headed by officials known as the Toiseach and the Mormaer, who corresponded roughly to the later posts of Thane and Earl. They, in turn, owed allegiance to the Sub-Kings and the High King.

One of the distinguishing features of this early culture was that land was held in common, administered on behalf of all by the tribal leader. As Scotland was exposed to influences from the south, however, the basic structure of government was altered. In particular, feudalism was introduced, a system which was based on the ownership of land. The process began during the reign of Malcolm III (1058-1093) and accelerated under David I (1124-1153), when many

CRUACHAN FROM GLEN NANT *Cruachan Beann is the talismanic hill of the Campbells, to whom, at one time or another, nearly all the smaller kindreds paid tribute. 'Cruachan' was the war cry of the Campbells.*

Norman lords settled north of the border. Under feudal law, all land belonged to the king, which he then granted to his followers in return for fealty. In Scotland, however, a unique system emerged, which enabled feudalism and tribalism to coexist. A normal feudal relationship was maintained between the sovereign and the various clan chiefs while, within the clan, the old order managed to survive.

In essence, the clan was run along the lines of an extended family. Indeed, the word (*clanna*) means 'children' in Gaelic. In this context, the chief was the father of his people. He settled their disputes, protected them from their enemies, and led them in battle. In return, he wielded absolute authority over them. After the chief, the most important person was the tanist. It was his duty to protect the interests of the clan for posterity. Where there were disputes about the succession of the chiefship, these were settled by the laws of tanistry. On rare occasions, this could mean that a direct heir was passed over, in favour of a more powerful warrior or astute leader.

LOCH MAREE *A stunning Scottish landscape, Slioch mountain looks over Loch Maree. In 1607 the abundant pine and oak at Loch Maree tempted Sir George Hay to exploit the region's forests for the manufacture of iron.*

The internal make-up of the clan followed a broadly consistent pattern. It was usually composed of 'native men' and 'broken men'. The former were blood-relations of the chief, while the latter were outsiders, granted the protection of the clan. As the community grew, it would be sub-divided into different septs or branches. These were headed by prominent members of the clan – often the younger sons of a chief. They exercised authority over their own people, though they still acknowledged the overall leadership of their 'father'.

The cohesion of the clan was strengthened by a number of social practices. Fosterage was commonplace. Children (not necessarily orphans) were frequently reared in the households of other families, to ensure that clan loyalties were as strong as blood ties. Handfasting was another widespread custom, which allowed couples to live together for a year and a day and then part, by mutual agreement, if they failed to have children. In addition, septs or followers of the clan could enter into bonds of manrent, which guaranteed mutual protection and assistance in times of trouble. Membership of the clan also entailed certain payments to the chief, most notably calps, which were roughly equivalent to death duties.

One of the weaknesses of the clan system was the propensity for feuding. Highlanders guarded their traditions fiercely and the slightest infringement of these could lead to bloodshed. Some disputes lingered on for centuries. Arguments over land were the most common source of conflict, but the causes could be comparatively trivial. At Culloden, for example, Jacobite morale was sapped by a bitter dispute between the MacDonalds and the Stewarts. As usual, the former claimed the honour of leading the right-hand flank. They had been granted this privilege at Bannockburn (1314) by Robert the Bruce, as a reward for sheltering him when he was a fugitive, and had held it ever since. Lord Murray, however, caused great dissatisfaction by conferring this position on the men of Atholl.

Despite problems of this kind, the organization of the clans proved a popular system, which endured for many centuries, until it was swept away by the failure of the Jacobites and the start of the Clearances. The key to its success lay in the fierce pride and loyalty, which the emphasis on blood-ties inspired. Each man could think himself a gentleman, a direct descendant of the distinguished ancestor, whose name he bore. 'Though I am poor, I am noble' ran a popular proverb of the MacLeans. It was a claim that could have been made by any other member of a Highland clan.

THE RIVER DEE *The majestic Dee rises in the heart of the Cairngorms and is one of the famous salmon rivers of Scotland. The name derives from the Gaulish word for goddess.*

Highland Dress

FOR MANY PEOPLE, tartan is the most evocative symbol of the Scottish nation. It is instantly recognizable and, even if some of the best-known designs are comparatively modern, its roots still lie deep within the country's past.

There is some controversy about the origin of the name. It probably derives from the French word *tiretaine*, although this refers to a type of woollen material rather than a pattern. The Gaelic word for tartan, *breacan* ('speckled'), is much more descriptive. The true sources of Highland dress are also open to question. Many authorities believe that it originated in Ireland, where there are medieval tomb effigies with figures wearing kilt-like garments. All are agreed, however, that the kilt itself is a fairly recent development and that Highlanders initially wore the belted plaid.

A KILT IN THE INNES TARTAN.
Kilts are sometimes also called philabegs.

commentators used to describe Highland dress as 'ancient Roman garb'.

The belted plaid had certain advantages. It could be worn in a variety of different ways, depending on the weather and the freedom of movement required. Sometimes, for example, the upper part of the plaid could be worn around both shoulders, like a cloak. Equally, when fighting, some Highlanders would wind the surplus material around their left arm, using it as a rudimentary shield. Finally, it provided the warrior with his bedding, a distinct advantage if he was seeking refuge in the wild from an English soldier or a rival clansman.

On the debit side, it could be cumbersome during hand-to-hand combat. There are many accounts of warriors throwing off their heavy plaids, fighting on in their shirts, and then scouring the battlefield later to recover their clothing. In addition, the plaid was unsuitable for riding and, from a very early stage, horsemen wore trews, a kind of trouser. This included the chief and his officers and, significantly, many early portraits depicted them in this attire (see page 92).

This plaid was a large, rectangular piece of material (in a Gaelic context 'plaid' refers simply to a blanket and has none of the modern, connotations with tartan). In order to don it, the clansman would first place it on the ground, with his belt underneath. He would then pleat it and lie down on top of it. Next, he would fold the cloth over him, buckle the belt and stand up. After putting on his coat, he would then loop the remainder of the cloth over his left shoulder and secure it in his belt. The effect was not unlike a toga and, indeed, early English

The kilt was essentially a smaller version of the plaid. It derives from the Danish word *kilte* ('to tuck up'), which describes the action of securing the material. In Gaelic, this was rendered as *filleadh*, and a distinction was soon made between the *filleadh mor* ('great kilt' or

'plaid') and the *filleadh beg* ('small kilt' or philabeg). No one knows precisely where or when the first kilt was worn, but there is little to suggest that it was much in use before the Jacobite uprisings. Ironically, one of the few known pioneers was an Englishman, Thomas Rawlinson. He owned an iron foundry in Glengarry and, in the early years of the 18th century, he introduced a version of the small kilt, believing that it would be more convenient for his workers. He is unlikely to have been the inventor of the garment, but the very possibility is enough to fill many Scots with horror.

The use of tartan designs on Highland dress is an equally vexed question. It seems probable that the earliest tartans indicated a region or district, rather than an individual clan. This was certainly the impression given by the traveller, Martin Martin, when he wrote about his experiences in 1695. The evidence for clan tartans is contradictory. In 1618, for example, Sir Robert Gordon of Gordonstoun is said to have written a letter to Murray of Pulrossie, asking him to remove the red and white lines from the plaids of his men, 'so as to bring their dress into harmony with that of the other septs'. Unfortunately, this letter has been lost and there is an abundance of evidence to suggest that Gordon's views went unheeded for more than a century.

In portraits predating the '45 Rebellion, many chiefs were depicted in tartans that bear no resemblance to their modern counterparts. The most striking example of this can be found at Castle Grant in Morayshire, which contains a series of ten family portraits in Highland dress. These were painted between 1713 and 1725 by the same artist, Richard Waitt, an itinerant English painter. Despite this, the tartans are all different and only two of them display any similarity to today's Grant tartan. The same point is made even more forcibly in David Morier's depiction of the Battle of Culloden. Here, the various clansmen are shown wearing different tartans on their hose, their jackets, and their plaids. Morier's picture is thought to be fairly accurate, since it was commissioned by the Government, which apparently allowed him to use Jacobite prisoners as models. These and other pictorial sources suggest that, while tartans were in widespread use, they had no special clan significance and were chosen at the personal whim of the wearer. The notion that they could be

SGIAN DUBH *The sgian dubh is a short knife, worn in the stocking. It did not become general wear until the 19th century.*

STEWART HUNTING (ABOVE) *The muted colours of hunting tartans can be worn at any time, whilst, in general, dress tartans are reserved for formal occasions.*

SHOES AND BELT Shoes should be low cut and, if they have ornamental buckles, these should match the design on the belt.

used as a form of identification seems to have stemmed from the introduction of regimental tartans. Attitudes to Highland dress were very mixed. In the Lowlands, both tartan and kilts were generally regarded with some distaste, as the garb of brigands, cattle thieves, and paupers. Echoes of this view were expressed by one 19th-century laird who, when asked if his family had a tartan, replied caustically 'Good gracious, no. My ancestors were always able to afford trousers'. Despite this, opinion started to shift after the fall of the Stuarts. Gradually, tartan began to acquire overtones of Jacobite or nationalist sympathies.

These sentiments were further sharpened by a growing list of grievances. After the expulsion of James VII (1688) and the false dawn of the victory at Killiecrankie (1689), Scots were appalled by the Massacre at Glencoe (1692), which was widely regarded as a brutal attempt by William III to quell any thoughts of rebellion in the Highlands. This was followed by the hugely unpopular Treaty of Union (1707), which effectively ruled out any hope of a peaceful return to Stuart rule. This, in turn, led to the two principal Jacobite uprisings (1715 and 1745).

After the 1715 rebellion, the Government tried to avert a recurrence of the problem by confiscating the weapons of the Highlanders. This proved ineffectual and, as a result, the measures taken after defeat at Culloden (1746) were much more severe. Their purpose was quite blatant: to dismantle the essential elements of Highland culture. At the heart of this legislation was the Dress Act (1747), which made it illegal for any male to wear Highland dress, 'that is to say, the plaid, *philabeg* or little kilt, trowse, shoulder belt or any part whatsoever of what peculiarly belongs to the Highland garb; and that no tartan or parti-coloured plaid or stuff shall be used for great-coats or for upper coats'. The penalty for this crime was six months' imprisonment or, for a second offence, transportation.

This Act remained in force for thirty-five years. Some clansmen found ingenious ways of getting round the regulations and some joined the army, where tartan could still be worn. By and large, however, it proved frighteningly successful. When the Act was finally repealed in 1782, the old traditions had been swept away. The tartans that delighted Sir Walter Scott and his contemporaries, and which are still in use today, had to be re-invented rather than rediscovered.

This process was inspired by the Celtic revival, which blossomed in the latter part of the 18th century. The Romantic movement, with its love of all things colourful and exotic, spawned a fascination with the remote and mysterious Highlands. Early hints of this can be found in the much-acclaimed

SOCKS Socks should obviously match the tartan of the kilt, although this did not always happen in the early days. This is an Innes pattern.

MCIAN ILLUSTRATION *This figure in full Fraser outfit comes from* Clans of the Scottish Highlands *(1845), compiled by the actor and illustrator Robert McIan.*

publication of Macpherson's poems about Ossian (1765), a mythical Scottish hero, and in Boswell's account of his Scottish tour with Dr Johnson (1785), but it was the novels of Sir Walter Scott which really captured the imagination. His tales about rebellious clansmen and Jacobite outlaws were just far enough in the past to qualify as adventure, rather than sedition.

The enthusiasm for Scottish culture was shared by England's king and, in 1822, George IV paid a royal visit to Edinburgh. The entire event was stage-managed by Scott, who wore a pair of Campbell trews for the occasion, and it reached its climax in a grand reception at Holyrood, where the king delighted his hosts by wearing a kilt of Royal Stewart tartan. The visit proved a great success and, needless to say, it prompted many Scotsmen to scurry off to their tailor, to find out about their own family tartan.

This was no simple matter, since very little information about the older tartans was readily available. The most reliable records had been kept by regimental weavers, such as Wilson's of Bannockburn, and, even here, many of the designs were numbered rather than named. As a result, clothiers would frequently attribute clan names as they saw fit, or else introduce their own patterns. To counter this, James Logan published *The Scottish Gael or Celtic Manners, as Preserved among the Highlanders* (1831), the first serious study on the subject, and important collections of verified tartan samples were put together by General Sir William Cockburn (1810-1820) and the Highland Society of London (*c*.1815-1816). At the other end of the scale, John Sobieski Stuart Hay and his brother – who claimed to be descended from Bonnie Prince Charlie – are thought to have fabricated many of the tartans in their book, the *Vestiarium Scoticum* (1842).

Logan's book contained just fifty-five tartans, but there are now several hundred in circulation. There are no overall controls on the wearing of tartan and, in practice, people can wear whichever pattern they prefer. Properly speaking, however, clans tartans should be worn only by men who can claim descent through the male line.

For everyday wear, Highland dress should consist of a kilt, a tweed jacket and waistcoat with horn buttons, plain brogues and knitted hose with garters, a leather sporran and 'Balmoral' bonnet. A *sgian dubh* ('black knife') may be worn in one stocking. For evening wear, the jacket should be of dress cloth or velvet, with short tails. There are kilts for ladies, but they should not wear sporrans. The correct attire is a pleated skirt or, in the evening, a skirt of tartan silk. A tartan sash may be worn, fixed by a brooch to the right shoulder.

JACOBITE SCREENS *Women often wore tartan screens (the old name for shawls) to display their Jacobite sympathies. This one bears a Sinclair design.*

The idea of incorporating tartan designs into official military uniforms dates back to the 18th century. It was first used in 1713 by the Royal Company of Archers, the Queen's Bodyguard for Scotland. A contemporary portrait of the 5th Earl of Wemyss shows that, initially, the uniform featured areas of bright red tartan on the jacket and trews. By the end of the century, when Raeburn painted his portrait of Dr Nathaniel Spens (*c*.1793), this had been replaced by a dark green tartan on the jacket alone. This colour has remained in use ever since.

The duties of the Royal Company of Archers were largely ceremonial until, after the first Jacobite uprising (1715), the Government decided to establish a group of small military corps to police the Highlands. Accordingly, in *c*.1729, Marshal Wade raised six Independent Companies for just this purpose. In theory, the recruits could be drawn from absolutely any part of the country, but most officers came from Whig clans, such as the Campbells, the Grants, and the Munros. Unlike the regular troops, who wore breeches and scarlet coats, these soldiers were attired in belted plaids. At this stage, each company adopted the tartan of its commander's clan.

The experiment proved a success and, in 1739, the Government added four new companies and turned the force into a regiment of the line. It was now necessary to select a single tartan for this new body and the authorities opted for a dark tartan composed of blue, green, and black stripes. Because of its sombre colouring, this became known as *Am Freiceadan Dubh* or the Black Watch. The belted plaid was still the order of the day – to be worn during reviews, guard-duty, and on active service. When the men were at leisure in their barracks, they wore kilts. For some reason, these were made of a different tartan, namely Murray of Atholl.

The official title of the new force was the 43rd (later the 42nd) Regiment, which was changed to the Royal Highland Regiment in 1758. Nevertheless, it was always popularly known as the Black Watch, and the design of its tartan was hugely influential. All but one of the later Highland regiments based their tartan upon it, as did many individual clans. A cursory glance at the setts of the Baillies, the MacLarens, and the Mackenzies will underline the similarities. By the same token, it is possible the Black Watch pattern was itself drawn from an earlier clan tartan. It is often claimed, for example, that it was identical to the original Campbell tartan, apart from the fact that it was dyed in darker shades.

During the 1745 rebellion, most of the Black Watch regiment was discreetly stationed in south-east England. Once the immediate danger was over, however, the Government was determined to send fresh troops to the north, to enforce the Disarming Act (1746). Ironically, they were able to recruit some of these from the Highlands themselves.

There were several reasons why this was possible. Many of the Jacobites, who had gone into exile or had their estates forfeited after the uprising, saw this as their best means of recovering their fortunes. By volunteering for military service, they hoped to secure a pardon

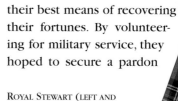

ROYAL STEWART (LEFT AND RIGHT) *Here, a Scots Guard wears the Royal Stewart tartan. It is also worn by other regiments, including the Black Watch and the Queen's Own Cameron Highlanders.*

or, alternatively, to earn the money to buy back their land. There was also another, equally compelling reason: it would enable them to bypass many of the restrictions in the hated Dress Act. For, soldiers were exempted from the general ban on wearing tartan. This helps to explain why, in the years following Culloden, the Government was able to raise nine new regiments, along with several companies of Fencibles.

Most of the new regiments based their tartan on the Black Watch pattern, but there was one notable exception. Alan Cameron of Erracht, the Colonel of the 79th Regiment (the Cameron Highlanders), was unwilling to dress his men in the Government sett (an alternative name for Black Watch). So, instead, his mother designed a new one for the clan. This resembled one of the MacDonald tartans. Pipers, too, were rarely clad in the regimental tartan. Most opted for Royal Stewart, though the Royal Highland Fusiliers came to use Erskine Dress.

Many of the new regiments were posted abroad, while the Fencible (short for 'defensible') corps remained in Scotland. These special units were akin to a Home Guard and were only raised for brief periods, in times of emergency. The notion of introducing them in the Highlands was first broached in 1759, when it was received with great scepticism. The '45 rebellion was still fresh in the memory, and many felt that companies of this kind would merely serve as a training ground for a new revolt. As a result, only the Duke of Argyll and the Earl of Sutherland – deemed the most reliable of the Highland lords – were permitted to raise Fencible regiments in 1759. During the Napoleonic era, however, when the threat of invasion was very real, the practice was extended to most areas. In all, there were twenty-six Fencible units in Scotland, most serving from the mid-1790s until 1802.

For the historian, military tartans provide an invaluable insight into the early development of Highland dress. Regimental weavers kept better records than many individual clans and despatched agents to

CAMPBELL (ABOVE) *This is thought by many to be the source of the Black Watch tartan.*
CAMERON OF ERRACHT (CENTRE) *This tartan is now used by the Queen's Own Cameron Highlanders.*
GORDON REGIMENTAL (RIGHT) *Dating from 1793, this can be distinguished from the other Black Watch setts by its single yellow stripe.*

the Highlands, to seek out authentic designs. The most important of these firms was William Wilson & Sons, who operated from Bannockburn. After *c.*1770, they enjoyed a near monopoly in supplying tartan for the army, and their pattern books offer the first written evidence of many well-known tartans.

Locating the Clans of Scotland

The intention of this map is to show approximate territories of the clans and families of Scotland. It is not always possible to include all the families on a small scale map like this. Therefore if a family is not included it does not necessarily imply that they were landless.

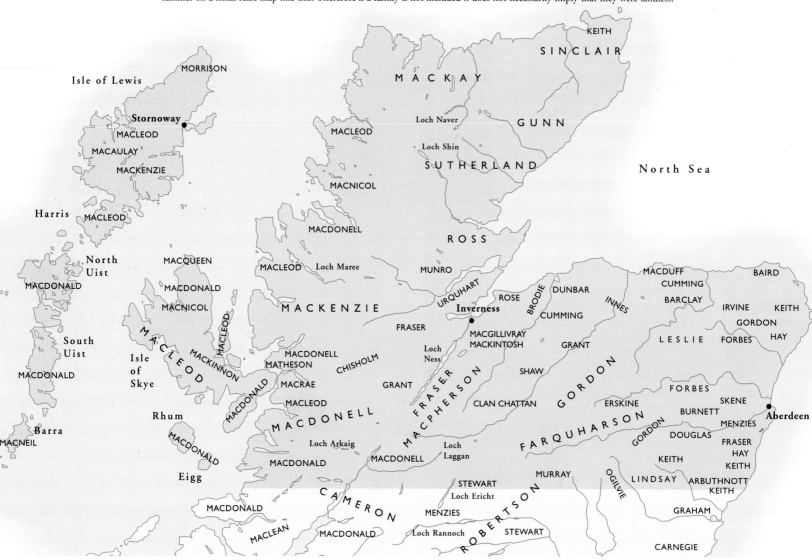

KEITH

SINCLAIR

MORRISON

Isle of Lewis

MACKAY

GUNN

Stornoway

Loch Naver

MACLEOD

MACLEOD

MACAULAY

Loch Shin

MACKENZIE

SUTHERLAND

North Sea

MACNICOL

Harris

MACLEOD

MACDONELL

ROSS

North
Uist

MACQUEEN

MACLEOD   Loch Maree   MUNRO

MACDUFF

BAIRD

CUMMING

MACDONALD

MACDONALD

URQUHART   ROSE   DUNBAR   BARCLAY

INNES

IRVINE   KEITH

MACNICOL

MACKENZIE

Inverness   CUMMING

GORDON

South
Uist

Isle
of
Skye

MACLEOD

FRASER

MACGILLIVRAY

LESLIE   FORBES   HAY

MACKINNON

MACDONELL

MACKINTOSH

GRANT

MACDONALD

MATHESON

CHISHOLM

Loch
Ness

SHAW

FORBES

MACRAE

GRANT

CLAN CHATTAN

SKENE

Rhum

MACLEOD

ERSKINE

BURNETT   MENZIES

Barra

MACDONALD

MACDONELL

FARQUHARSON

GORDON

DOUGLAS

FRASER

MACNEIL

Loch Arkaig

Loch
Laggan

MACDONALD

HAY

Eigg

MACDONALD

MACDONELL

KEITH   KEITH

STEWART

MURRAY

LINDSAY

ARBUTHNOTT

Loch Ericht

OGILVIE

KEITH

MACDONALD

CAMERON

MENZIES

ROBERTSON

GRAHAM

MACLEAN

MACDONALD

Loch Rannoch   STEWART

CARNEGIE

Aberdeen

Abercrombie

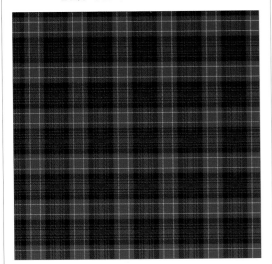

The Abercrombie sett was woven in a variety of colours. This version is from Logan (1831).

THE CLAN NAME is taken from the Barony of Abercrombie in Fifeshire. The earliest known holder of the title was William de Abercromby (1296) and this line of the family survived until the 17th century, when leadership of the clan passed to the Abercrombies of Birkenbog. Sir Ralph Abercromby commanded the Royal Highlanders in expeditions to Barbados (1796) and Egypt (1801). During the former, the Highland plaid was temporarily replaced by Russian pantaloons.

MURTHLY CASTLE *Murthly remained in Abercrombie hands until the early 17th century, when Sir William Stewart blackmailed them into selling it.*

Agnew

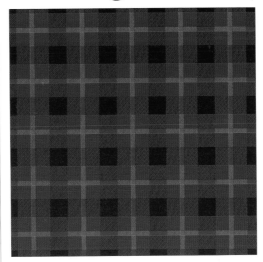

An attractive modern tartan, designed to unite the far-flung members of the Agnew clan.

CONTROVERSY SURROUNDS the origins of the Agnews. Most believe that they came from Norman stock, taking their name from the Barony d'Agneaux. According to this theory, the family settled in England after the Conquest (1066) and were first noted in Scotland in 1190. In that year, a certain William des Aigneu was cited as a witness on a charter from Jedburgh Abbey. Alternatively, the name may be an anglicized form of the Ulster sept of O'Gnimh (later O'Gnew). Either way, the Agnews established themselves in the Wigtown and Galloway region. They held the ancestral castle of Lochnaw and gained the hereditary post of Sheriff of Wigtown in 1451.

Allison

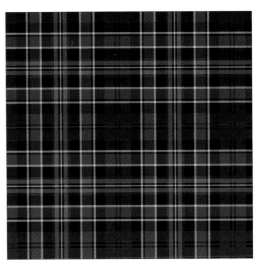

This tartan was included in the MacGregor-Hastie Collection (c. 1930–1950).

ALLISONS ARE usually cited as a sept of either the MacAlisters or the MacDonalds. The name itself may have several derivations. It is most commonly defined as 'Son of Alice', although 'Son of Ellis' is equally probable. It may also be a variant of Allanson ('Son of Allan'), but this is less likely. Its use as a female forename became widespread in the 15th century, probably as a result of the popularity of the romance of Abelard and Héloise (or Aloyse), and the name may have been brought home by Scottish archers in the French army. Early documented examples include Patrick Alissone, who signed the Ragman Rolls (1296), and Peter Alesoun, who was a witness in Brechin (1490).

Anderson

*A sample of this pattern was received by the
Highland Society of London in c.1815.*

LITERALLY, THE NAME means 'son of Andrew', a reference to Scotland's patron saint. Anderson is more common in the Lowlands, while the Highland version is MacAndrew. The latter, thought to have originated as a sept of the Clan Chattan, flourished in Aberdeenshire. The most notorious member of the clan was Iain beag MacAindrea (John MacAndrew), whose skills as a bowman were legendary. In 1670, a group of 'cattle-lifters' descended on Badenoch and spirited away the laird's herd. MacAndrew was among the pursuers, tracking them down to a tiny bothy. There, he fired off his arrows with such unerring accuracy that all but one of the raiders were killed.

Angus

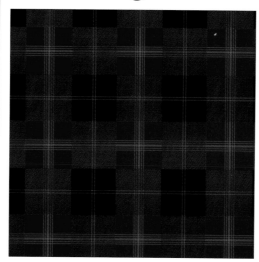

*A comparatively modern tartan, this design was
first recorded by Johnston (1906).*

THIS TARTAN IS associated with both the district of Angus and the family surname. The word means 'the one and only', and may well refer to one of Scotland's founding fathers. Oenghus (the Irish form of Angus) was a 6th-century ruler of Dalriada. He belonged to a branch of the ancient Scots and, together with his father and two brothers, he founded the settlement of Dalriada in Argyll. Although often threatened with extinction, the people from this tiny kingdom eventually migrated eastwards, forming the core of the future Scottish nation. Angus is often linked with the Clan MacInnes (literally 'Son of Angus'), who also claim descent from the Dalriada Scots.

Arbuthnott

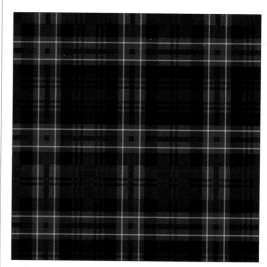

*Registered with Lord Lyon in 1962, this is based
on the Black Watch tartan.*

DERIVED FROM the clan's ancestral lands in Kincardineshire, in its earliest form, the name was written as 'Aberbothenoth' ('mouth of the stream below the great house'). Both the name and the estates were assumed by Hugh of Swinton and his heirs, who were granted them by Walter Olifard, in the late 12th century. Perhaps the best-known family member was Dr John Arbuthnot (1667–1735), who was born in Kincardineshire and studied at St. Andrews, before seeking his fortune in England. There, he made his mark as a political satirist, much admired by Pope and Swift.

Armstrong

A Lowland tartan, first recorded in the Sobieski brothers' book Vestiarium Scoticum *of 1842.*

LEGEND SUGGESTS that the name of Armstrong has a very literal origin. For, it was bestowed upon Fairbairn, a royal armour bearer, after he had used his strength to rescue the king in battle. The monarch also rewarded his servant with estates in Liddesdale, in the Borders. In time, the Armstrongs became a powerful, warlike faction in this area, often dubbed as 'reivers' ('robbers'), because of their frequent raids into England. The Armstrongs can also claim to be the most travelled of the clans, as one of their descendants was the astronaut Neil Armstrong, who carried a fragment of the tartan with him, during his moon-walk.

Baillie

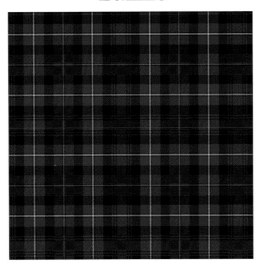

One of the tartans from the pattern books of Wilson's of Bannockburn (1819).

BAILLIE COMES FROM the post of bailie or bailiff, which usually refers to a magistrate, although it can be applied more loosely to any royal officer. Several notable families are associated with the clan, among them the Dochours, the Polkemmets, and the Lamingtons. The tartan itself was one of the military patterns used by the regimental weavers, Wilson's of Bannockburn. In 1797, it was confirmed as the sett worn by the Baillie Fencibles. These Fencibles (short for 'defensible') were an early form of Home Guard, designed to counter the threat of Napoleonic invasion. Most of the military tartans were closely modelled on the Black Watch pattern.

Baird

This sett was recently modified, with the triple-stripes now woven in purple, rather than red.

THE NAME STEMS from a variant of the word 'bard' or poet, but the reasons for this association are no longer known. By tradition, the founder of the clan was a follower of William the Lion, who saved his master's life during a boar hunt. The king rewarded him with lands and a title. The family is first recorded in Lanarkshire but, by the 14th century, the Bairds were more prominent in the Lothians and Aberdeenshire. The clan crest depicts an eagle's head, perhaps as a reference to one of Thomas the Rhymer's prophecies. This foretold that when the eagles nesting on the estate disappeared, the Bairds would lose their ancestral home.

Barclay

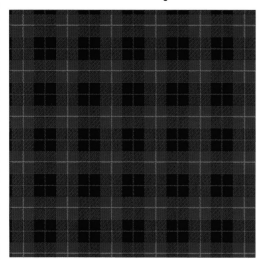

The Barclays' hunting sett first appeared in the Vestiarium Scoticum *(1842).*

OF NORMAN DESCENT, the Barclays trace their line back to the followers of William the Conqueror. Roger de Berchelai ('beautiful field') and his son John are thought to have arrived in Scotland in 1067, as part of the retinue of the future Queen Margaret. After her marriage to Malcolm III, she granted them the lands of Towie. Many of their descendants attained high office. In 1165, Sir Walter de Berkeley held the post of Chamberlain of Scotland, while Sir David Barclay was a close associate of Robert the Bruce. More distinguished still was the Russian Field Marshal, Michael Andreas Barclay, who was created Prince Barclay de Tolly for his part in the defeat of Napoleon (1812).

Baxter

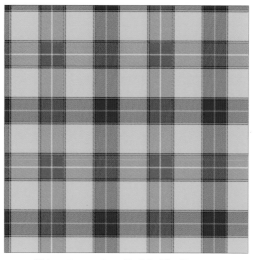

This sett was described in The Baronage of Angus and Mearns *(1856).*

BAXTER IS an archaic word for a baker and, as with many names relating to occupations, this one is found throughout Scotland. Even so, the greatest concentrations were in Fife and in the west. In the latter, the Baxters were generally regarded as dependents of the Macmillans. In Fife, by contrast, a separate branch had gained prominence by the 13th century. Reginald Baxter witnessed a document relating to Wemyss church in c.1220, while Jeffrey le Baxtere of Lissithe gave an oath of fealty in 1296. The principal family in the area, however, was the Baxters of Earlshall, who resided in a fine baronial mansion near Leuchars.

Borthwick

The clan that uses this tartan probably takes its name from Borthwick Water in Roxburghshire.

SOME BELIEVE THAT the family came over with Caesar's legions, others that they stem from Celtic roots. Certainly, they can be linked with the Saxon party, who escorted Margaret Aetheling to her marriage with Malcolm III. The family rose to prominence in the 15th century, when the first Lord Borthwick was created and the redoubtable Borthwick Castle was erected (1430). Here, Mary Queen of Scots took refuge, following her marriage to Bothwell. The castle was immediately surrounded, but Mary escaped, dressed as a page-boy. The Borthwicks' support for the Royalist cause continued through to the Civil War, when the 11th Lord was one of the last to surrender to Cromwell.

Bowie

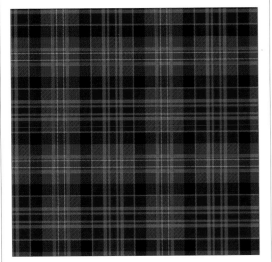

*This tartan belongs to a family regarded
as a sept of the MacDonalds.*

ALTHOUGH SOME Bowies incorporated archery motifs into their crests, the origins of the name are probably related to farming. 'Bow' was an old term for cattle (from the Latin *bos*, which is also the root of bovine) and the surnames of Bowie and Boe were often interchangeable (the latter is a much attenuated form of 'bullock'). Alternatively, the name may have come from the Gaelic word *buidhe*, meaning 'yellow' or 'fair-haired'. In Strathspey, the Bowies were counted as followers of the Grants. There are several other variants of the name, most notably Boye, Boee, Bouie, and MacIlbowie.

Boyd

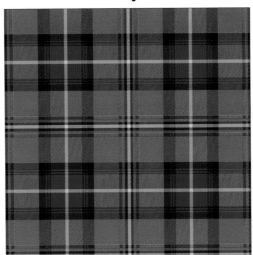

*The Boyd tartan was designed for Lord
Kilmarnock and registered in 1956.*

THE ORIGINS OF the name are much disputed. There are theories that it came from *Bhoid*, the Gaelic word for the island of Bute, or, like Bowie, from *buidhe* ('fair' or 'yellow'), referring to the hair colour of the clan's founder. Others claim that the word is more likely to be Norman, since the first Boyds came from across the Channel. In the 12th century, the sons of the Hereditary Steward of Dol settled in Scotland and, a century later, Robert de Boyte was among the noblemen who signed the Ragman Rolls (1296), confirming his allegiance to Edward I. The clan has always had strong links with the town of Kilmarnock, and the 10th Lord Boyd was created Earl of Kilmarnock in 1661.

Brodie

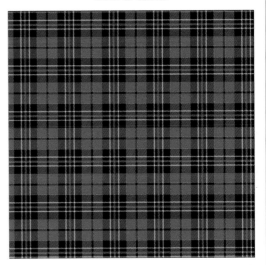

*The Brodies used to wear the Huntly tartan,
but had switched by 1850.*

AN ANCIENT FAMILY, BRODIE may well date back to Pictish times, when many of the kings were called Brude. There was also a thanedom with the same name in Morayshire, and Michael Brodie of Brodie was confirmed in this title by Robert the Bruce, shortly before Bannockburn. The most notorious of the later family members was Deacon Brodie, who concealed his criminal activities behind the façade of a respectable town councillor. Eventually, however, he was caught trying to rob the Excise Office in Edinburgh. He was hanged in 1788, on a set of gallows that he had designed himself and persuaded the council to approve.

BRUCE SEE PAGES 24–25

Bruce

OREVER LINKED WITH the exploits of Robert the Bruce, this famous clan sprang from a powerful Norman family. They probably took their name from the castle of Brix, near Cherbourg, which was built by Adam de Brus in the 11th century. Robert de Brus participated in William the Conqueror's invasion of England and was rewarded with property in Surrey and Yorkshire. His son, also Robert, was in the service of the future King David I and, upon his succession (1124), travelled north to claim the lands of Annandale. This, however, did not entirely end the Bruces' involvement in English affairs, for in 1138 father and son fought on opposite sides at the Battle of the Standard, near Northallerton.

The family's rise to the throne began in the mid-13th century, when Robert, 4th Lord of Annandale, married Isabella of Huntingdon, niece of William the Lion and great-granddaughter of David I. This gave them a realistic claim to the Crown in 1290 when, with the death of Queen Margaret ('the Maid of Norway'), the House of Dunkeld became extinct. In all, there were thirteen claimants to the throne, though the main contest lay between John Balliol and Robert the Bruce. Initially, Edward I threw his support behind the former, believing that he would be the most amenable candidate. Using his rights as a feudal lord over Balliol's English estates, he attempted to bring Scotland under his personal control. Then, when Balliol resisted, Edward invaded Scotland (1296), stripped the new king of his crown, and carried away the stone of Scone. He also forced the defeated Scottish nobility to swear fealty to him, by signing the Ragman Rolls (so-called because the cluster of seals gave the documents a ragged appearance).

With the removal of Balliol, the mantle of resistance passed briefly to William Wallace. Then, after his execution (1305), it was transferred to John 'the Red' Comyn, Balliol's nephew, and Bruce. Their rivalry

ROBERT THE BRUCE *Robert the Bruce was Scotland's greatest hero. He had himself crowned at Scone in 1306, but it was only after the victory at Bannockburn (1314) that he could feel truly secure. He ruled as Robert I until 1329.*

BRUCE (BELOW) *This tartan was first recorded in the* Vestiarium Scoticum *(1842), although it is thought to be much older.*

BRUCE HUNTING (RIGHT)
This sett was manufactured by Peter Anderson of Galashiels in c.1939.

ROBERT THE BRUCE STATUE *This modern statue shows Robert the Bruce sheathing his sword after the Battle of Bannockburn. It is situated on Stirling Castle's esplanade, which commands a fine view of the battlefied.*

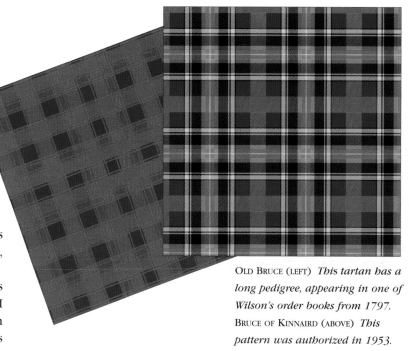

OLD BRUCE (LEFT) *This tartan has a long pedigree, appearing in one of Wilson's order books from 1797.* BRUCE OF KINNAIRD (ABOVE) *This pattern was authorized in 1953.*

came to a head in 1306, when the pair met at Greyfriars Church, in Dumfries. A quarrel ensued and Bruce stabbed Comyn to death. This rash gesture forced him to gamble and so he went to Scone and declared himself king. At this stage, however, he was regarded as little more than an outlaw and his first clash with the English (Methven, 1296) resulted in a humiliating defeat.

For the next few months, Bruce was a fugitive, until the death of Edward I (1307) presented him with a golden opportunity. The new English king, Edward II, did not inherit his father's military skills and, in any event, was absorbed with problems at home. Bit by bit, Bruce gathered support and waged war on his Scottish enemies – the kinsmen of Comyn and their allies, the MacDougalls. Over the years, his strength increased, so that his next great showdown with the English (Bannockburn, 1314) proved an unmitigated success.

Although this secured his position, Bruce had to battle for years to win formal recognition from his foes. Peace with the English was achieved only in the Treaty of Northampton (1328), signed just a year before his death. Similarly, his long-running dispute with the papacy, which had excommunicated him in 1310, was also finally resolved in 1328. Bruce was delighted and announced that, after his death, he wished his heart to be carried on a crusade against the infidel. His request was fulfilled and, in 1330, Sir James Douglas took his

embalmed heart to Spain, during his campaign against the Moors. Bruce's heart was later buried in Melrose Abbey, while his body was interred at Dunfermline.

Robert was succeeded by his son, David II, who ruled Scotland from 1329–1371. He died childless, however, bringing to an end the short-lived House of Bruce. After this, the Crown passed to the first of the Stewart kings, Robert II, who was descended from Bruce through the female line. Robert the Bruce's younger brother, Edward, was also briefly a monarch, occupying the Irish throne from 1316–1318. The Bruces later gained the title of Earl of Elgin (1633) and are thereby related to Thomas, 7th Earl of Elgin, the noted archaeologist who brought back the Elgin Marbles from Athens (1816).

Buchan

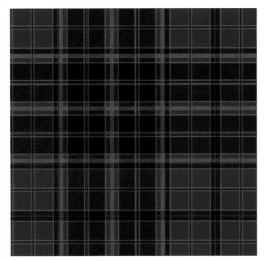

*The oldest surviving sample of this tartan
dates back to 1790.*

THE BUCHANS TAKE their name from a stretch of land in Aberdeenshire, extending from the River Don to the River Deveron. This was governed by the Mormaers (later, the Earls) of Buchan. By the 12th century, this had come into the hands of the Comyn family, thus beginning the long association between the Buchan and Cumming clans. Their most famous kinsmen are Alexander Buchan (1829-1907), the meteorologist and John Buchan (1875-1940), the novelist and statesman. Who, although most celebrated for his five Richard Hannay thrillers, particularly *The Thirty-Nine Steps* (1915), later became Governor General of Canada, earning the title of Baron Tweedsmuir.

Buchanan

*A sample of the Buchanan tartan was donated
to the Highland Society of London (c.1815).*

ANSELAN O'KYAN, an Ulster chief, was thought to have been granted the lands of Buchanan by Malcolm II in *c*.1016, in recompense for his services against the Vikings. These lands lay to the north and east of Loch Lomond and probably had some connection with the church, for the name derives from *Both-chanain* ('the Canon's Seat'). It is recorded that Gilbert, the seneschal of the Earl of Lennox, adopted the name in the mid-13th century, when he acquired the estate from his master. Notable members of the clan included James Buchanan (1791-1868), 15th President of the United States, and George Buchanan (1506-1582), tutor to Mary Queen of Scots.

Burnett

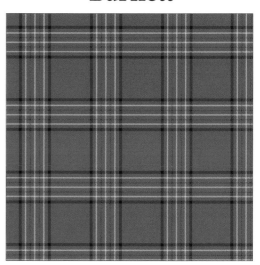

*This is the Burnett of Leys tartan. The family have
strong connections with Robert the Bruce.*

THE BURNETTS claim descent from one of the great Anglo-Saxon families of England. The Burnards (originally Beornheard, 'brave warrior') travelled to Scotland in the train of Matilda of Huntingdon, who married King David I in 1114. They were granted land at Fairnington in the Borders. The family remained strong supporters of the Scottish Crown and, after Bannockburn, Robert the Bruce gave them part of the Forest of Drum, on Deeside. He also offered them the magnificent Horn of Leys, which still resides in Crathes Castle, their ancestral home. In 1626 Sir Thomas Burnett was created Baronet of Nova Scotia, for his promise to help found a Scottish colony in the Americas.

Burns

A modern tartan dating from c.1930. There is a separate Robert Burns pattern.

THE FAMILY ARE generally associated with the Campbells. Their surname is of territorial origin and is linked with several locations, both in England and Scotland. During the reign of Edward I (1272-1307), there was a lord by the name of Burnes in Burneshead, Cumberland. Similarly, the Bernes family held lands of the same name in Glenbervie in c.1329. The name may ultimately derive from the word 'burn' ('a brook'). Robert Burns (1759-1796), Scotland's most celebrated poet, was actually born with the name 'Burnes' and was the first member of his family to drop the 'e'.

CAMERON SEE PAGES 28–29,
CAMPBELL SEE PAGES 32–33

Carmichael

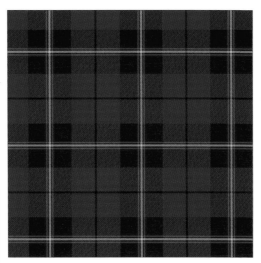

A comparatively modern tartan, delivered to the Highland Society in 1907.

THE CARMICHAELS take their name from a barony in upper Lanarkshire, which was part of the Douglas estates. The family is documented from 1226, when Robert de Carmichael was cited in a charter of Dryburgh Abbey but it was in the following century that they acquired the Carmichael lands from William, Earl of Douglas. The Carmichaels became known for their military prowess, none more so than Sir John de Carmichael, who fought with the French against English invaders. In 1421, at the Battle of Beauge, he unseated Henry V's brother, the Duke of Clarence, shattering his spear in the process. As a result, a broken spear became the focal point of the Carmichael crest.

Carnegie

A variant of the tartan used by the MacDonells of Glengarry.

JOCELYN DE BALLINHARD, a 13th-century lord is usually cited as the founder of this clan. In 1358, his descendant, John de Ballinhard, acquired the estates of Carryneggy, near Arbroath. The direct line died out in 1563, when leadership of the clan passed to the Carnegies of Kinnaird, who owned land near Brechin. The family were fervent Royalists, and Sir David Carnegie was made Earl of Southesk in 1633. The 2nd Earl accompanied Charles II into exile, where he gained a more dubious reputation as a practitioner of the black arts. More recently, Andrew Carnegie (1835-1918) founded the Pittsburg steelworks and used his immense fortune to endow libraries and universities.

Cameron

THE CAMERONS ARE an ancient clan, proud of their reputation for being 'fiercer than fierceness itself'. Their name comes from the Gaelic *Cam-shron*, which describes a 'hooked' or 'crooked nose'. Initially, there were three separate branches: the MacSorleys of Glen Nevis, the MacMartins of Letterfinlay, and the MacGillonies of Strone. Up until the start of the 16th century, these were organized like a confederation rather than a clan, with a captain at their head.

The acknowledged ancestor of the Camerons was Donald Dubh, who was born in *c*.1400. He married the heiress of the MacMartins and united the various families under the banner of the Clan Cameron. Donald's younger son, Allan, founded the line of the Camerons of Strone. Allan, in turn, was followed by his son Ewen. Under his leadership, the lands of Lochiel were converted into a barony (1528) and he became the first Cameron to include them in his name. Ewen married twice, and one of the children from his second marriage became the ancestor of the Camerons of Erracht.

CAMERON (BELOW) *First illustrated in the Sobieskis'*
Vestiarium Scoticum, *published in 1842.*

CANNON *This cannon is one of the exhibits at the Clan Cameron Museum, located at Achnacarry House.*

CAMERON HUNTING (RIGHT)
According to a contemporary account, this is the tartan worn by the Camerons at the Battle of Killiecrankie (1689).

Ewen was also the great-grandfather of Taillear Dubh na Tuaighe ('Black Taylor of the Axe'), a redoubtable warrior. Taillear's ancestry explains the close links between the clans of Cameron and Taylor. Many of his descendants adopted the name of Cameron Taylor.

The clan's best known figure was Sir Ewen Cameron of Lochiel, 17th Chief, who was born in 1629. He was orphaned at an early age and was raised by the Marquis of Argyll, who tried to instil the principles of the Covenanters into him. Ewen was more inspired by the exploits of Montrose, however, and, after witnessing his execution in Edinburgh (1650), he became a determined Royalist. In 1652, he joined the Earl of Glencairn, who had raised the royal standard in the Highlands, and took part in a series of skirmishes against the English. In particular, he harried the forces of Generals Monk and

SIR EWEN OF LOCHIEL (BELOW) *A strong supporter of the Stuarts.*

CAMERON OF LOCHIEL (ABOVE) *Taken from George Chalmers' portrait of the Gentle Lochiel (1764).*

Morgan, who were trying to enforce Parliament's rule in the area. Soon, his deeds acquired a legendary aura. Supporters of the Stuarts revelled in the popular tale of how, when he was engaged in a hand-to-hand struggle with one Cromwellian officer, Ewen had bitten away his opponent's throat.

Ewen was eventually compelled to submit (1654), but his reputation won him very favourable terms. He did not have to make any personal oath of allegiance to Cromwell, he was granted compensation for the damage done to his property at Lochiel, and he and his men were granted immunity from prosecution for their actions. After the Restoration, Ewen was received in London by Charles II and was granted a knighthood in 1680.

The chief's fighting days were not yet over, however, for in 1689 he took the field at Killiecrankie. He was now sixty years old, and had been offered both money and a title for his neutrality, but Ewen's commitment to the Stuart cause was total. He also gave his full support

to the 1715 rising although, in this instance, the clan was led by his son. Ewen died four years later, at the age of ninety.

After Ewen, the most illustrious Cameron was his grandson, Donald, who became known as 'the Gentle Lochiel'. He had the misfortune to be Chief of the clan at the time of the '45 rising. After Bonnie Prince Charlie landed in Scotland, Lochiel met with him and urged him to return to France, to await a time when he had better support. The Prince refused, however, uttering his famous reply – that if Lochiel did not wish to join him, he could stay at home and learn about his fate in the newspapers. Reluctantly, Cameron gave way and joined the rebellion. It proved to be a disastrous decision. He was wounded at Culloden and forced to flee to France, where he died in 1748. In his absence, the Cameron lands were forfeited and their houses burned to the ground.

LOCH ARKAIG *The Camerons acquired the lands of Loch Arkaig in 1528, when James V granted them to Ewen of Lochiel.*

29

Chisholm

This sett was listed in the Vestiarium
Scoticum *of 1842.*

THE CHISHOLMS were of Norman stock and were first recorded in Roxburghshire, in the Borders. In 1254, John de Chesehelme was mentioned in a papal bull, while a Richard de Chesehelme featured in the Ragman Rolls of 1296. During the 14th century, the Chisholms gained greater influence in the north, when they became Constables of Urquhart Castle on Loch Ness. The family became supporters of the Jacobite cause, and clan members were actively involved in both uprisings (1715 and 1745).

GLEN AFFRIC *After Culloden, Hugh Chisholm helped Bonnie Prince Charlie find shelter in a cave in Glen Affric.*

Christie

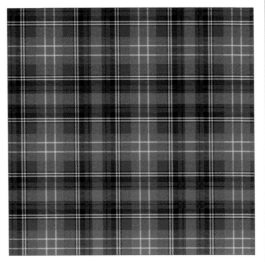

Two versions of this modern tartan were presented to the Scottish Tartans Society.

ALTHOUGH TRADITIONALLY associated with the Farquharsons, the origin of this family name is uncertain. It may derive from an Old Norse word applied to a swordsman (*thrysta*, meaning 'thrust'), but it is more likely to be the diminutive of a forename. Christian, Cristinus, and Christopher are all possibilities. The name is particularly common in the Fife and Stirling areas, where the earliest references date from the 15th and 16th centuries. In 1457, John Chrysty was cited as a burgess in a charter drawn up by the Abbot of Lindores, while Jhone Cristie was described as a 'burne ledder' (water carrier) in St. Andrews (1590).

CLAN CHATTAN SEE PAGE 36

Clark

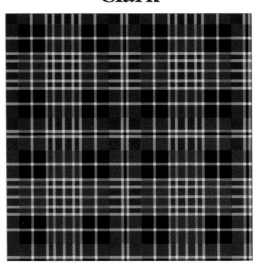

This sett was featured in the pattern books of Wilson's of Bannockburn (c.1819).

THE NAME HAS an ecclesiastical origin. It derives from the Latin word *clericus*, which means both a 'cleric' and a 'clerk'. Inevitably, families with this name are found in most parts of Scotland, although the principal links are with the Cameron, Macpherson, and Mackintosh clans. The tartan is sometimes known by the name of Clergy or Priest. The earliest known references date from the 12th century, when Roger Clericus was cited as a landowner. Notable family members include Richard Clark, a native of Montrose, who rose to become a vice-admiral in the Swedish navy (1623), and George Rogers Clerk, who was one of the earliest settlers northwest of the Ohio.

Campbell

TRADITION LINKS THIS family with Diarmid Ua Duibhne ('Diarmid of the Love Spot'), a romantic hero of Irish legend, and for many years it was known as the Clan Duibhne or the Clan Diarmid. The first Campbell, it is said, married Eva O'Duibhne, Diarmid's descendant. This tradition is very old – it was confirmed in a charter of 1368 – and it does feature one intriguing coincidence. The name 'Campbell' is almost certainly derived from the Gaelic *cam-beul* ('crooked mouth'), and the father of the mythical Diarmid was Fergus *Cerr-beoil* ('wry mouth').

Despite all this, the first documentary evidence of the clan dates from 1263, when Gillespie Campbell was mentioned in a charter. Then, in 1292, Sir Colin Campbell of Lochawe was cited as one of the greatest lords of Argyllshire. He is generally recognized as the founder of the Campbells of Argyll, and the Gaelic form of his name – *Cailean Mor* – has been incorporated into the title of all subsequent chiefs.

Sir Colin was slain by one of the MacDougalls of Lorne in 1296, but the clan began to prosper under the chiefship of his son, Sir Neil. He was a loyal supporter of Robert the Bruce and, as a result, was rewarded with extensive territories in the west Highlands. The clan's

CAMPBELL (BELOW) *In use from the early 18th century, the Campbell tartan may also have been worn by the Highland Companies in 1725.*

CAMPBELL OF BREADALBANE (BELOW) *One of three different Breadalbane setts, used by Wilson's of Bannockburn (1819).*

LOCH AWE *The view in the distance shows the Pass of Brander, where Bruce and the Campbells defeated the MacDougalls in 1308.*

influence in the region was further increased, as the Crown strove to dominate the Lords of the Isles – first the Norse and then the MacDonalds. As a result, the Campbells became the leading power in the area by the close of the 15th century.

The clan has many important branches. The Campbells of Inverawe were descended from Neil's younger son, while both the Loudoun and Strachur lines stemmed from Sir Colin. After the House of Argyll, however, the leading branch of the family was the Campbells of Breadalbane. They were descended from Black Colin of Glenorchy, the second son of Sir Duncan Campbell of Loch Awe. He became a Lord in 1445 and his grandson, Colin, was created Earl of Argyll in 1457. Sir John Campbell, 11th of Lord Glenorchy, was made Earl of Breadalbane in 1681. The family also came to hold the thaneage of Cawdor, famous from Shakespeare's *Macbeth*. The founder of this line was another Sir John Campbell, the third son of the 2nd Earl of Argyll. He forged the link to the title through his marriage to Muriel, daughter of Sir John Calder (1510). The Cawdor estates eventually passed to their grandson, who sold most of them, so that he could acquire the island of Islay.

The clan entered a difficult period in the 17th century. Many of the chiefs were Protestants, which complicated their relationship with the Stuart kings. Archibald, 8th Earl of Argyll, also known as 'Gloomy Archibald', was a prominent supporter of the Covenanters and this eventually led to his execution. His son, the 9th Earl, suffered the same fate, for taking an active part in Monmouth's Rebellion of 1685 (an attempt to overthrow James VII). The Campbells fared better, however, under England's Protestant kings. In 1703, the 10th Earl was elevated by William III to the Duke of Argyll and Marquess of Lorne. The 2nd Duke became Commander-in-Chief of the British army and, in 1746, four companies of the clan – 'my brave Campbells', as Cumberland described them – fought for the English at Culloden.

The most controversial incident in the clan's history is, of course, the Massacre at Glencoe. On a February night in 1692, thirty-eight members of the MacDonald clan were killed in their beds by a detachment of Campbell troops, led by Robert Campbell of Glenlyon. The atrocity shocked all Scotland, although the Campbells might point out in their defence that they were merely settling old scores. For, the MacDonalds of Glencoe had assisted Montrose in 1644, when he carried out particularly brutal raids against the Campbells.

ROBERT CAMPBELL OF GLENLYON *He led the soldiers who carried out the infamous Massacre at Glencoe in February 1692.*

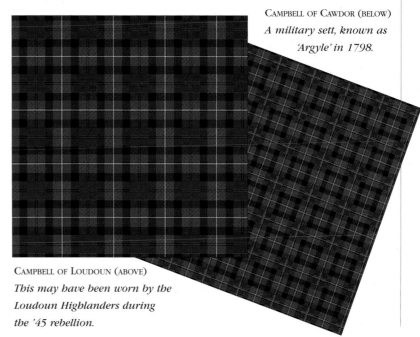

CAMPBELL OF CAWDOR (BELOW) *A military sett, known as 'Argyle' in 1798.*

CAMPBELL OF LOUDOUN (ABOVE) *This may have been worn by the Loudoun Highlanders during the '45 rebellion.*

Cochrane

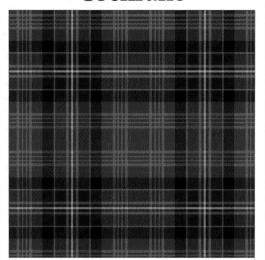

*Dating from 1934, this sett is based on
the Lochaber district tartan.*

LEGEND HAS IT that the founder of the Cochrane clan was a Viking raider who settled in Renfrewshire in the Early Middle Ages. More certainly, the name derives from the lands of Coueran, near Paisley. In 1262, Waldeve de Coveran witnessed a charter relating to the Earl of Menteith. Similarly, in 1296, William de Coveran signed one of the Ragman Rolls. The family rose to greater prominence in the 17th century, when William Cochrane was made Earl of Dundonald. In time, the clan chiefs became known as 'the fighting Cochranes', because of their military exploits. The greatest of them was the 10th Earl (1775-1860), who commanded the navies of Chile, Brazil, and Greece.

Cockburn

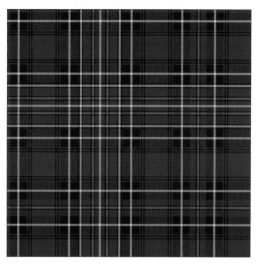

*The Cockburn tartan was in use during
the Napoleonic era.*

THE NAME appears to come from a property near Duns, in Berwickshire. The Cockburns themselves are first mentioned as vassals of the Earls of March, but their fortunes improved in the 14th century, when David II bestowed the Barony of Carriden on Sir Alexander de Cockburn. Later family members appear on the fringes of Scottish history. One was Keeper of the Great Seal of Scotland, while another, Admiral Cockburn, escorted Napoleon to St. Helena. The most distinguished figure was Henry Cockburn (1779-1854), the Whig politician and judge. He rose to the post of Solicitor-General in 1830 and played a leading role in drafting the Scottish Reform Bill (1832).

Colquhoun

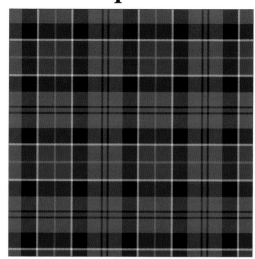

*A sample from Paton's collection (1830s), with
purple in place of the traditional blue.*

A TERRITORIAL NAME, deriving from the Barony of Colquhoun in Dunbartonshire. The founder of the clan, Humphrey de Kilpatrick, acquired the lands from the Earl of Lennox during the reign of Alexander II (1214-1249). The Colquhouns were longstanding enemies of the MacGregors, even more so after their defeat at Glenfruin (1603). Strong connections in the USA developed, where prominent members included John Calhoun (1782-1850), who became American Vice-President, and Lieutenant Jimmy Calhoun, who fell at Custer's last stand.

LOCH LOMOND *The clan's ancestral lands lie by the shores of Loch Lomond.*

Clan Chattan

UNIQUE AMONG THE Scottish clans, this was not a single family but a confederation of different clans, grouped together for mutual protection. There are a number of conflicting theories about the origin of the name, but it probably derives from Gille Chattan Mor, whose name means 'Great Servant of St Cathan'. The latter had been one of St Columba's companions and Gille Chattan was a baillie at Ardchattan Priory, which was dedicated to him.

Initially, the Chattans held land around Loch Arkaig and Glenloy, and functioned like a conventional clan. Then in 1291, Eva, the only child of Dougall Dall, 6th Chief, married Angus, 6th Laird of Mackintosh. They moved to the traditional Mackintosh estates at Rothiemurchus and Angus assumed the title of Captain of Clan Chattan. The clan expanded rapidly, until a host of different families claimed membership.

In essence, Clan Chattan was composed of three separate strands: those families which traced their line back to Gille Chattan Mor (the Cattanachs, the Macphails, the Macphersons, and the MacBains); those who belonged to Mackintosh or one of its offshoots (the Farquharsons of Invercauld, the Shaws of Tordarroch, the Ritchies, the Mac-Thomases of Finegand); and an assortment of

CHATTAN CHIEF (RIGHT) This sett is reserved for the chief and his immediate family. It was approved by Sir Aeneas Mackintosh of that ilk in 1816.

other clans, which had no blood relationship with Clan Chattan, but which sought its protection (the MacGillivrays, the MacQueens of Pollochaig, the MacIntyres of Badenoch, the Davidsons, the MacLeans of Dochgarroch, the Gows, the Clarks).

The sheer size of the clan gave it a powerful voice in Highland affairs for several centuries although, inevitably, there were disputes about its leadership. For more than two hundred years, the chiefs of the Macphersons argued that they should be captains of the clan, since they were descended from Muireach, a great-grandfather of Eva. Their claim was finally dismissed by Lord Lyon in 1672.

Persuading the confederation to speak with a single voice on contentious issues proved an even thornier problem. As a result, the clan convened special meetings, where members tried to settle their differences by swearing Bonds of Union. Despite this, the wounds re-opened during the Jacobite disturbances. In 1745, for example, the Captain of Clan Chattan (a Mackintosh chief) was an officer in George II's army and did not respond to Prince Charlie's call. Instead, his wife selected MacGillivray of Dunmaglass as the Chattan commander.

In the aftermath of Culloden, the links between the clans were sorely weakened and the confederation was effectively dissolved. Nevertheless, the chiefs of the Mackintoshes continued to head Clan Chattan until as recently as 1947.

CHATTAN (LEFT) Similar to the chief's tartan, apart from the single white line.

Connel

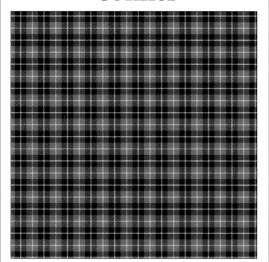

*This is probably based on the Wallace
tartan, which dates from c.1842.*

BOTH THE CONNELS and MacConnels are recognized as septs of the Clan Donald. The name probably has an ecclesiastical origin, deriving from one of the missionary saints in early Scottish history. The likeliest figure is St Comgall (died *c.*601), who is thought to have been a warrior before taking orders. Comgall spent most of his career in his native Ulster, but he is also associated with St Columba on Iona and is said to have accompanied him on his mission to Brude, King of the Picts. Alternatively, the name may have come from St Congual, a more obscure figure who was linked with Dercongal (later Holywood) in Dumfriesshire.

Cranstoun

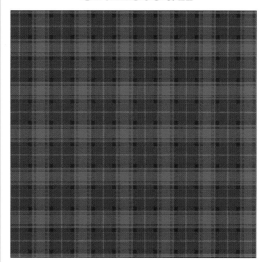

*This is the tartan of one of the Lowland clans,
based in Roxburghshire and Midlothian.*

AN ANGLO-SAXON origin is claimed for the name of Cranstoun, which may be translated as 'the place of the crane'. Despite this, the founder of the clan was a 12th-century Norman, Elfric de Cranston, whose name appears on a charter belonging to the Abbey of Holyrood. The Cranstons fell out of favour briefly during the 16th century, when some were accused of treason, as a result of their support for the Earl of Bothwell, and one, Thomas Cranston, was executed in 1600 for his role in the Gowrie Conspiracy. Despite this, Sir John Cranstoun of Morristoun was raised to the peerage in 1609, following his appointment as James VI's Captain of the Guard.

Crawford

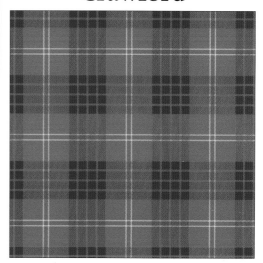

*This tartan may have been designed by the
Sobieski brothers in the early 19th century.*

THE NAME IS of territorial origin, deriving from the Barony of Crawford in Clydesdale. Early records (1179) refer to Galfridus de Crawford, but the first concrete information about the family dates from 1248, when the death of Sir John Crawford of that ilk was noted. He had two daughters, the younger of whom married David Lindsay of Wauchopedale, the ancestor of the Earls of Crawford. A cadet branch of the family produced Margaret Crawford, wife of Sir Malcolm Wallace and mother of William, Scotland's patriotic hero. Other main branches were the Crawfords of Auchinames, so-called after the property bestowed on them by Robert the Bruce, and the Crawfords of Kilbirnie.

Cumming

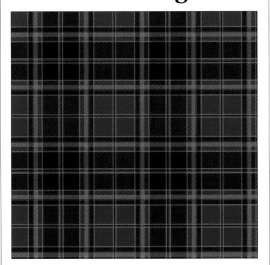

First illustrated in McIan's The Clans of
the Scottish Highlands *(1845).*

Robert de comyn, a follower of William the Conqueror, came from Commine, near Lille, which is the probable source of the family name. Robert's grandson settled in Scotland, where the clan rapidly became a powerful force. By the 14th century, the Comyns held four earldoms - Atholl, Menteith, Badenoch and Buchan. In 'Red' Comyn, Lord of Badenoch, they also had a serious contender for the Scottish Crown, until he was murdered by Robert the Bruce in a Dumfries church (1306).

RUTHVEN BARRACKS *These ruins, in the district of Badenoch, stand on the site of a former Comyn stronghold, which was seized by Robert the Bruce.*

Cunningham

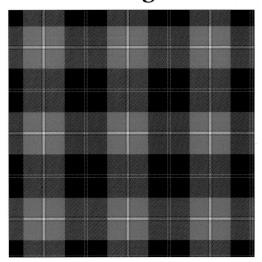

Similar to the tartan of the MacGregors, who were closely linked with this clan.

Wernibald, who settled in the Cunningham district of Ayrshire in *c.*1140, is usually cited as the ancestor of the clan. A century later, his descendant, Hervey de Cunningham, was granted the lands of Kilmaurs by Alexander III, as a reward for his valiant service at the Battle of Largs (1263). The Kilmaurs remained the principal branch of the family, gradually adding the estates of Lamburgton, Finlaystoun, and Glencairn to their possessions. Alexander de Cunningham was made Earl of Glencairn by James III in 1488. The 14th Earl was a close friend of Robert Burns and, after his death in 1791, the poet wrote the moving *Lament for the Earl of Glencairn.*

Dalziel

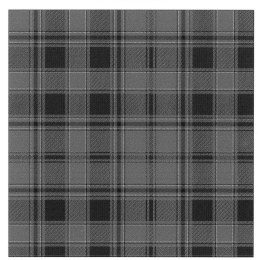

This pattern was used for a George IV tartan, in honour of the monarch's visit (1822).

The name derives from the Barony of Dalzell, in Lanarkshire. In Old Scots, the literal meaning of the word is 'I dare', and this has become the motto of the clan. The family was first recorded in 1288, when Hugh de Dalzell held the post of Sheriff of Lanark, and his descendants eventually procured the earldom of Carnwath (1649). The best known family member, however, comes from a junior branch, the Dalzells of Binns. This was headed by General Thomas Dalzell (1599-1685), who was nicknamed 'the Muscovite Devil' because of his military exploits for the Tsar. On his return to Scotland, he formed a famous regiment of dragoons, the Royal Scots Greys (1681).

Davidson

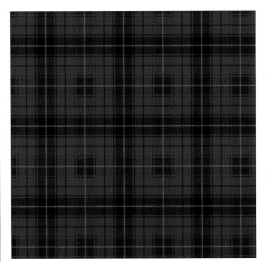

This pattern, dating from 1893, omits the white stripe of earlier versions.

IT SEEMS THAT the Davidsons were originally a sept of the Comyns, until their power began to wane in the 14th century. They transferred their allegiance to the Mackintoshes, thereby becoming part of the Clan Chattan Confederation. Within the Clan Chattan, they became involved in a fierce feud with the Macphersons over rights of precedence. This led to the bitter battle on the North Inch of Perth (1396) when the two clans virtually destroyed each other. Subsequently, the principal branches of the clan were the Davidsons of Cantray and the Davidsons of Tulloch.

DOUGLAS SEE PAGE **43**

Drummond

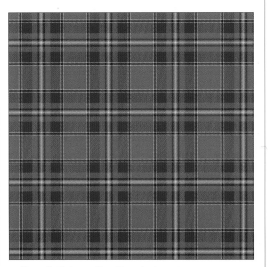

Bonnie Prince Charlie is believed to have worn this tartan during the '45 Rebellion.

DRYMEN, IN STIRLINGSHIRE, is where the clan takes its name from. Its founder was Malcolm Beg, who was steward to the Earl of Strathearn in 1225. One of his descendants, Sir Malcolm de Drymen, fought alongside Robert the Bruce at Bannockburn and is said to have scattered the caltrops (metal spikes), which disabled the English cavalry. Two Drummonds have been queens of Scotland. Margaret, daughter of Sir Malcolm, married David II in 1363. He divorced her when she failed to bear him a child, but Margaret appealed to the papacy and had the decision reversed. Similarly, Annabella Drummond became the wife of Robert III and mother of the future James I.

Dunbar

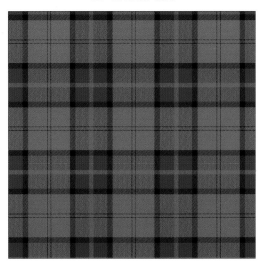

A Lowland tartan, first recorded in the Vestiarium Scoticum of 1842.

THE DUNBARS TRACE their line back to Crinan, the Thane and Seneschal of the Isles and the father of Duncan I, the murdered king in Shakespeare's *Macbeth*. Dunbar Castle, the family seat, occupied a strategic position close to the English border. Accordingly, it was besieged on many occasions, most notably in 1337 when 'Black Agnes', the wife of the 9th Earl, defended it successfully for several months. The most distinguished family members were Gavin Dunbar, who held the post of Lord Chancellor during the reign of James V, and William Dunbar (*c*.1465–*c*.1530), the poet sometimes hailed as the 'Scottish Chaucer'.

Duncan

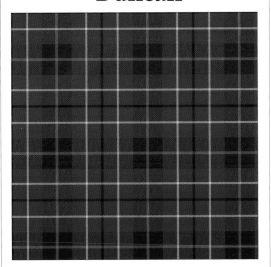

Deriving from the Gaelic words donn *and* cath, *Duncan, means 'the brown warrior'.*

THE HISTORY OF the Duncans and the Robertsons is closely intertwined, since both are descended from the ancient Earls of Atholl. They shared the name 'de Atholia' until the 14th century, when Donnachadh Reamhar ('Fat Duncan') distinguished himself at the Battle of Bannockburn. The principal estates of the Duncans were in Forfarshire, where they held the Barony of Lundie. This branch of the family produced Sir William Duncan, personal physician to George III, and Adam Duncan, who became an admiral in 1795. Two years later, he achieved a stunning victory over the Dutch fleet at Camperdown and was created Viscount Duncan of Camperdown by King George IV.

Dundas

This elegant pattern was included in the Sobieski brothers' famous book of tartans.

SERLE DE DUNDAS, the traditional founder of this prominent Lowland clan, lived during the reign of William the Lion (1165-1214) and owned lands bearing the family name on the shores of the Forth. Serle's descendants were actively involved in the struggle against the English. Sir Hugh fought alongside Wallace, while his successor was a staunch ally of Robert the Bruce. After the Union, however, the family became loyal servants of the Crown. Chief among them was Henry Dundas, 1st Viscount Melville, who acted as William Pitt's principal agent in the North, earning the nickname of 'the uncrowned king of Scotland'.

Dyce

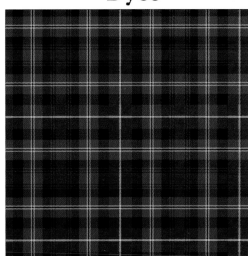

This is the tartan of an Aberdeenshire family who are linked with the Skenes.

THE NAME HAS a territorial origin, deriving from the lands of Dyce near Aberdeen (the city's airport is now located there). The earliest record dates from 1467, when John de Diss was confirmed as a burgess of Aberdeen. The family has strong artistic associations. Alexander Dyce (1798-1869) was a noted Shakespearian scholar from Edinburgh. His nine-volume edition (1857) of the plays was a standard work and his library was donated to the Victoria & Albert Museum. William Dyce (1806-1864) was a painter, designer, and educationalist. His *Pegwell Bay* (1859-1860) is one of the finest examples of Pre-Raphaelite landscape painting.

Douglas

ALTHOUGH ONE of the most famous Scottish families, the origins of the Douglases are surprisingly obscure. The name means 'Black Stream' in Gaelic (*Dubh-Glas*) and may refer to one of their early territories. The first documentary evidence dates from the end of the 12th century, when William de Douglas witnessed charters relating to Kelso Abbey. His descendants fought at the Battle of Largs (1263) and the siege of Berwick (1296), but it was under Bruce that the family came to prominence.

Sir James Douglas, founder of the Black Douglases, was a key figure in the struggle for independence, his adventures forming the basis of Walter Scott's *Castle Dangerous* (1832). After Bruce's death, Sir James dutifully carried out his promise to take the king's heart on crusade against the Moors in Spain. Douglas was killed in action in Andalucia (1330), but Bruce's heart was rescued and taken to Melrose Abbey.

James's nephew, William, was created Earl of Douglas in 1357 and later became the Earl of Mar through marriage. The 2nd Earl of Douglas died at Otterburn (1388), while the 4th Earl married a daughter of Robert III and was a regent during the infancy of James II. The later history of the family was less auspicious. The 6th Earl was murdered at the so-called 'Black Dinner' (1440) and the earldom was forfeited in 1455.

The chiefship passed to the Red Douglases, the Earls of Angus, who became a powerful force. The 6th Earl, married the widow of James IV and proclaimed himself guardian of the infant James V. In 1633, the 11th Earl became a Marquess, but this title, along with the earldom of Angus, later devolved on the Dukes of Hamilton.

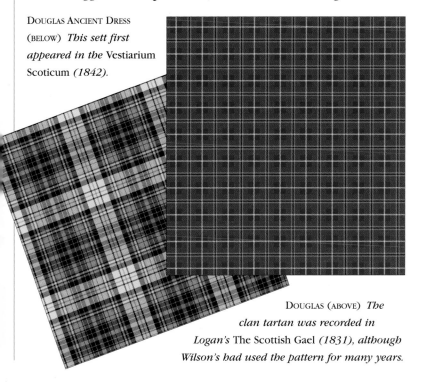

DOUGLAS ANCIENT DRESS (BELOW) *This sett first appeared in the* Vestiarium Scoticum *(1842).*

DOUGLAS (ABOVE) *The clan tartan was recorded in Logan's* The Scottish Gael *(1831), although Wilson's had used the pattern for many years.*

THREAVE CASTLE (RIGHT) *Built by Archibald the Grim, 3rd Earl of Douglas, Threave was notorious for its 'Gallows Knob' over the entrance.*

LOCH LEVEN (OPPOSITE) *Mary Queen of Scots was held prisoner in Loch Leven Castle (1567-1568) by Sir William Douglas. His son helped her to escape by locking his family in the hall and throwing the keys into the loch.*

Elliot

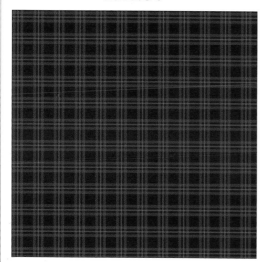

Originally spelt 'Elwold', the Elliot clan, who use this tartan, was based in the Borders.

CHIEF FAMILY in the clan, the Elliots of Redheugh date back to the 15th century. One of their number was Captain of Hermitage Castle, while Robert Elliot took part in the disastrous defeat at Flodden (1513). The Redheugh fortunes declined in the 17th century, however, when much of their land passed to the Elliots of Stobs. One of the lines which sprang from the Stobs' branch of the Elliots was the Minto family, which included some eminent statesmen. Sir Gilbert became Governor General of Bengal (1807-1813), while the 4th Earl served as Governor General of Canada.

Elphinstone

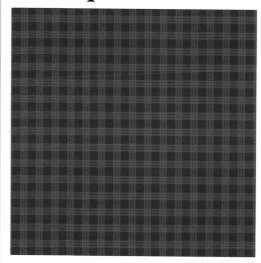

This tartan was first recorded in the Vestiarium Scoticum of 1842.

FIRST DOCUMENTED reference to this family occurred in a deed of 1235, where mention was made of John de Elfinstun. Then, almost a century later, one of his relatives married Margaret of Seton, Robert the Bruce's niece. The first clan member to make a major, historical impact, however, was a churchman, William Elphinstone (1431-1514). He became Bishop of Aberdeen in 1484, combining this with the role of Chancellor of Scotland. He was also instrumental in obtaining the foundation bull for Aberdeen University from Alexander VI. Later Elphinstone worthies include Alexander, 4th Lord, who became Lord High Treasurer, and John, 13th Lord, appointed Governor of Madras.

Erskine

A symmetrical pattern, which closely resembles the Cunningham and MacGregor tartans.

THE CLAN NAME derives from the Barony of Erskine in Renfrewshire and can be traced back to the 13th century. The family was related to Robert the Bruce and numbered itself among the trustiest of his supporters. It later came to acquire the earldom of Mar, one of Scotland's most ancient titles, and the earldom of Kellie. The Erskines rose to high office, none more so than John, the 6th Lord, who acted as Regent during the childhood of Mary Queen of Scots.

BRAEMAR CASTLE *Erected in 1628 by John Erskine, 2nd Earl of Mar, Braemar was soon under attack from his mortal enemies, the Farquharsons, and passed into their hands in 1732.*

Ferguson

THE FERGUSON CLAN IS widely dispersed throughout Scotland and it is likely that the various branches are descended from several different Ferguses. In the west, many clansmen claim Fergus Mór, son of Erc, as their ancestor. This shadowy figure was an ancient chieftain of the Scots, who founded the kingdom of Dalriada in the early 6th century. According to some, he also brought across with him from Ireland, the Stone of Destiny, Scotland's coronation stone.

Another popular theory, meanwhile, suggests that the clan was descended from a 12th-century Prince of Galloway. This Fergus built up a fearsome reputation, through his frequent rebellions against Malcolm the Maiden (Malcolm IV), although he is also credited with the foundation of Dundrennan Abbey.

The oldest known branch of the clan are the Fergusons of Kilkerran, based in Ayrshire, who probably acquired their lands in the 12th century. John, son of Fergus, signed a charter for Edward Bruce in c.1314, while Fergus, son of Fergus received land in Ayrshire from Edward's brother. Either of these may have been the ancestor of John Ferguson of Kilkerran, who was cited in a document of 1464. The Kilkerrans supported the Royalist cause during the Civil War and reached high office in the following century. Sir John Ferguson became one of the Nova Scotia Baronets in 1703 and was appointed judge of the Supreme Court in 1735. His descendant, Sir Charles, 7th Baronet, enjoyed a distinguished military career, before becoming Governor General of New Zealand.

Further north, the principal branch of the clan were the Fergusons of Dunfallandy. They originated in Atholl, taking their name from their estates near Pitlochry. Members of the clan were listed in the Act of Suppression (1587) and the family clashed with authority again during the Jacobite risings. In Dumfriesshire, the Fergusons of Craigdarroch were the principal line, tracing their history back to the reign of David II (1329-1371). In Aberdeenshire, meanwhile, the chief families were the Fergusons of Kinmundy, Baddifurrow, and Pitfour.

The clan has produced several other memorable figures. Robert Ferguson (1637-1714) became known as 'the Plotter', following his conspiracies against the Stuart kings, while Adam Ferguson (1723-1816) served in the Black Watch, before making his name as a philosopher and historian. Most celebrated of all, however, was the tragic young poet, Robert Fergusson (1750-1774). He created a vogue for verses in the Scots vernacular and was an important influence on Robert Burns. Above all, he wrote about Edinburgh, his native city, dubbing it *Auld Reekie* in his most famous poem. At the age of twenty-four, however, he was afflicted by a profound religious melancholy and died in a lunatic asylum.

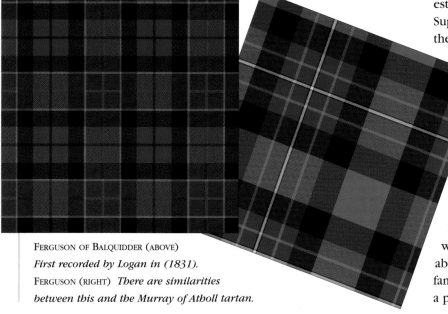

FERGUSON OF BALQUIDDER (ABOVE)
First recorded by Logan in (1831).
FERGUSON (RIGHT) *There are similarities between this and the Murray of Atholl tartan.*

Farquharson

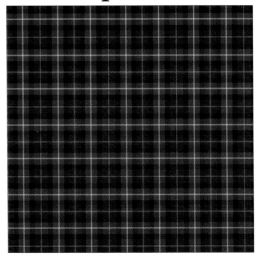

*The oldest surviving examples of this tartan
date back to 1774.*

THIS HIGHLAND CLAN owes its name to Farquhar, the son of Alexander Ciar, the 3rd Shaw of Rothiemurchus. Through the Shaw connection, it also belongs to the Clan Chattan, an ancient federation of tribes. The Farquharsons excelled as soldiers. Finlay Mor, for example, was the royal standard-bearer at the battle of Pinkie (1547), where he lost his life. Then, in the 18th century, they became fervent supporters of the Jacobite cause, taking part in the battles of Preston, Falkirk, and Culloden. Indeed, one of their number gained notoriety as the 'Black Colonel', whose deeds were celebrated in many Deeside ballads.

Fletcher

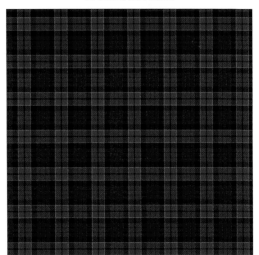

*Dating from 1906, this is similar to the
Old Lochaber district tartan.*

A FLETCHER IS AN arrow-maker and, consequently, the surname can be found throughout Scotland, since individual fletchers attached themselves to whichever clan was using their arrows. However, the Fletchers had particular associations with Achallader in Glen Tulla, which they held for many generations, and with Glenorchy, where they claimed to be the first inhabitants. From the main branch, the Fletchers of Saltoun, came Andrew Fletcher (1653-1716). He was a member of the Scottish Parliament in the turbulent years leading up to the Act of Union (1707), arguing vociferously for the continued independence of his country.

FORBES SEE PAGES **48–49**

Forsyth

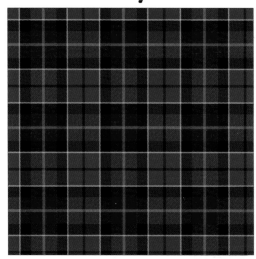

*Apart from its yellow stripe, this closely
resembles the Leslie tartan.*

IT HAS BEEN suggested that the name stems from the Gaelic word *Fearsithe* ('Man of Peace'), but this is uncertain. The family is not recorded until 1296, when Robert de Fauside added his name to the Ragman Rolls, thereby pledging his allegiance to Edward I. Despite this, Robert's son, Osbert, was given lands at Sauchie, in Stirlingshire, by Robert the Bruce (*c.*1306) and fought alongside him at Bannockburn. In more recent times, William Forsyth (1737-1804) was a noted horticulturalist, specializing in the cultivation of fruit trees. The *Forsythia* shrub was named after him.

FRASER SEE PAGES **50–51**

Forbes

THE NAME ORIGINATES FROM the Braes of Forbes, in Aberdeenshire. A colourful legend tells how the ancestor of the clan, Ochonochar, won possession of the land by killing a bear that had been terrorizing the district. These rights were confirmed in a charter of 1271, when the estate was converted into a barony. Alexander de Forbes was a fierce opponent of Edward I, losing his life at the siege of Urquhart Castle (1303), while his son perished at the Battle of Dupplin (1332).

The clan rose to prominence in the 15th century, largely through the activities of Sir John Forbes of the Black Lip and his four sons. The eldest of these, Alexander, fought at the Battle of Harlaw (1411) and was later created a peer (c.1445). His younger brothers, meanwhile, founded the Pitsligo, Polquhoun, and Skellater branches of the family. Alexander himself had three sons, the youngest of whom was ancestor of the Baronets of Craigievar.

During the 16th century, the clan became embroiled in long-running feuds with their traditional enemies, the Leslies and the Gordons. The struggle against the latter was particularly bloody, culminating in the battles of Tillieangus and Craibstone (both 1571), and in the pillaging of the Forbes' homes at Dumminor and Corgarff. Eventually, Parliament had to intervene, to bring the feuding to a close.

The Forbes owned many strongholds, but they are most closely associated with Craigievar and Castle Forbes, two of Scotland's most striking buildings. Craigievar, a stunning seven-storey tower, was completed in 1626 for William Forbes, the prosperous merchant better known as 'Danzig Willie', while Castle Forbes was built by the 17th Lord and is still the principal family seat.

CORGARFF CASTLE *Scene of an horrific attack on the Forbes by the Gordons in 1571. While the laird was absent, they set fire to the castle, killing his entire family and household.*

FORBES ANCIENT (BELOW) *This sett was registered at Lyon Court in 1949.*

FORBES (LEFT) *This sett was used by Wilson's of Bannockburn (1819).*

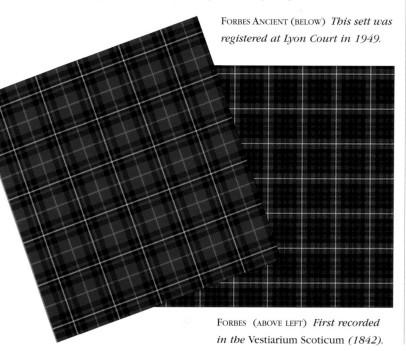

FORBES (ABOVE LEFT) *First recorded in the* Vestiarium Scoticum *(1842).*

Fraser

THE CLAN IS THOUGHT to come from French stock. Various places in Anjou and Normandy have been cited as possible sources for the name, most notably Fresles and Freselière, and it has even been suggested that they are descended from an earlier Gaulish tribe, which had a strawberry plant (*fraisier*) as its emblem.

The first documentary evidence dates from *c.*1160 when Simon Fraser granted land to the Abbey of Kelso. Several of his descendants fought alongside Bruce, in the struggle for independence. Sir Alexander of Touch was Bruce's chamberlain and married his widowed sister, Mary. She had suffered cruelly at the hands of the English,

FRASER HUNTING (RIGHT) First recorded by Johnston in 1906 although it may have been designed fifty years earlier.

FRASER (BELOW) The most popular of the clan tartans, this pattern was used by Wilson's of Bannockburn (1819).

being dangled in a cage from the walls of Roxburgh Castle for four years. Alexander was awarded the Thaneage of Cowie (1328), but later perished at the Battle of Dupplin (1332).

Alexander's brother, Simon, founded another important branch of the family, the Frasers of Lovat. This is thought to have come about through his marriage to the heiress of the Bisset estates, near Beauly, although the earliest written reference to a Fraser of Lovat dates only from 1367.

The Frasers of Philorth were responsible for the creation of Fraserburgh, in Aberdeenshire which stemmed from an ambitious scheme to transform the tiny port of Faithlie into a bustling town. The first charter was granted in 1546 and the project continued for many years, even though it virtually bankrupted the family. The Frasers did acquire a new title, however, when the 9th Lord of Philorth married the Saltoun heiress, becoming 10th Lord Saltoun in 1670.

While the Philorths were wrestling with their financial problems, the Frasers of Lovat were engaged in bitter feuding with the MacDonalds of Clanranald. In 1544, this culminated in the Battle of Blar-na-Leine ('the Field of Shirts'), when the warriors of both sides are said to have thrown off their heavy plaids, in order to fight more freely. In later years, the most infamous of the Lovats was Simon, 11th Lord, who was popularly known as the 'Old Fox' of the '45. He played false with both sides during the uprising, and was beheaded on Tower Hill for his pains – the last man to suffer this fate in England. So many people gathered to watch, that a stand collapsed, killing several spectators.

CAIRNBULG CASTLE Originally called Philorth, the clan acquired this doughty castle in 1375, when Sir Alexander Fraser married Joanna, daughter of the 5th Earl of Ross.

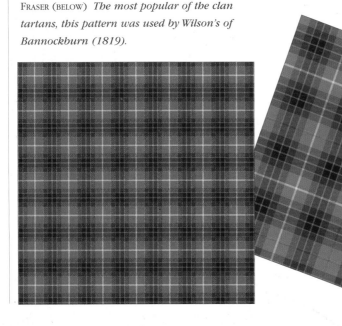

Galbraith

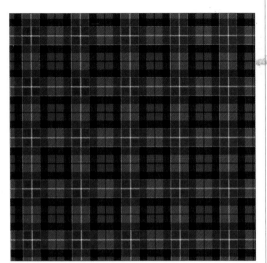

A sample of this tartan was listed in the collection of the Highland Society of London (c.1815).

THE NAME DERIVES from the Gaelic for 'foreign Briton'. The Britons had established a kingdom in Strathclyde by the 6th century, and the family ancestor may well have migrated from there into Celtic territory. In *c.*1208-1214, Gillescop Galbrath witnessed a charter by Malduin, son of the Earl of Lennox. The family appear to have been related to this noble for, in another document, Gillescop was cited as Lennox's nephew. Hugh de Galbrath was Provost of Aberdeen in 1342 but, in modern times, the most celebrated family member is J.K. Galbraith (b.1908), the Canadian economist. He has been a professor at Harvard, as well as US ambassador to India.

Gillies

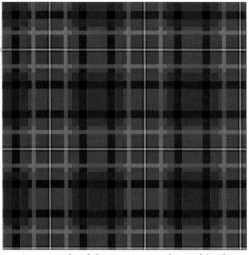

An example of this tartan was housed in the MacGregor-Hastie Collection (c.1930-1950).

THIS IS ONE of many Scottish surnames with an ecclesiastical background. It means 'Servant of Jesus' (*Gille Iosa*), which confirms that the ancestor was probably a monk or a church official. The family were followers of the Macphersons, and the name was most common in Badenoch and the Hebrides. In *c.*1128 a member of the Gillise family witnessed a charter granted by David I to Holyrood Abbey. Some years later, a son of Gillise witnessed another charter, relating to the Abbey of Scone (1164). More recently, Sir William Gillies (1898-1973) held the post of President of the Royal Scottish Academy.

GORDON SEE PAGE **53**

Gow

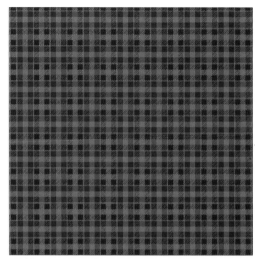

This tartan is featured in Raeburn's portrait of Niel Gow (c.1793).

GOW IS DERIVED from *Gobha*, the Gaelic word for blacksmith or armourer. Consequently the surname was widely dispersed throughout Scotland. Even so, there appear to have been close connections with the Macphersons in Clan Chattan, while links with the MacGowan ('Son of the Smith') clan are more obvious. Niel Gow (1727-1807), the fiddler and composer, toured Scotland for more than fifty years, delighting audiences with his hornpipes, reels and strathspeys. He was also fêted in the aristocratic circles, claiming the Duke of Atholl as his patron. Raeburn painted him in a striking pair of knee-length, tartan trews.

GRAHAM SEE PAGE **56**, GRANT SEE PAGES **54–55**

Gordon

THE CLAN NAME HAS a territorial origin, deriving from the lands of Gordon in Berwickshire. The family itself is thought to have Anglo-Norman roots, although a definite line of descent has not been established. The earliest documentary evidence dates from *c.*1155, when Richard de Gordun made a grant to the monks at Kelso. The power of the Gordons was concentrated in the Borders until the advent of Robert the Bruce. Sir Adam de Gordun served him as a Warden of the Marches and as a negotiator with both the English king and the papacy. For these services, Robert gave him the lands of Strathbogie in Banffshire, thus beginning the clan's long association with the north-east.

The Gordons' power increased considerably in the 15th century. Sir Alexander Gordon was made a lord in 1436 and his son became Earl of Huntly in 1449. They were also known by a less formal title, 'Cock of the North', which emphasized their immense influence throughout the region. On a more tangible level, this was reflected in the glorious Renaissance palace, which was erected at Huntly between 1597 and 1602. By this stage, the chief had gained the title of Marquess (1599), which was later elevated to a dukedom (1684). A separate branch, the Gordons of Methlick, became Earls of Aberdeen (1682).

Many famous figures have borne the name of Gordon. The 4th Earl of Aberdeen became British Prime Minister (1852–1855), while General Gordon will always be associated with the siege of Khartoum (1884–1885). George Gordon, 6th Lord Byron, was also linked with the Gordon clan. His mother was Catherine, one of the Gordons of Gight and the poet was raised in Aberdeenshire, after his father abandoned the family.

GORDON REGIMENTAL (LEFT) *In 1793, this sett was chosen for a new set of uniforms for the Gordon Highlanders.*

RED GORDON (RIGHT) *This sett, also known as 'Old Huntly', is sometimes used as the Huntly district tartan.*

HADDO HOUSE *Designed in 1731 by William Adam, to replace the House of Kellie – home to the Gordons of Methlick – which had been destroyed by Covenanters in 1644.*

Grant

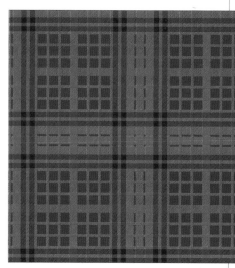

THE ORIGINS OF THE clan are much disputed. The most common explanation is that the Grants were Norman and that the name came from the French word for 'great' (grand). In this or in its Latin form (*magnus*), it crops up frequently in medieval documents. Despite this, there is also a longstanding tradition that the Grants were distant descendants of Kenneth MacAlpin.

The first recorded ancestor of the clan was Laurence le Grand, who held the post of Sheriff of Inverness in 1263. By this stage, the family already owned lands in Stratherrick, adding new territories in Glenmoriston and Glen Urquhart during the reign of Robert the Bruce. In 1493, the Grant lands were converted into the Barony of Freuchie and, in 1694, they were upgraded to a Regality. This unusual honour enabled the Grant Chiefs to rule like monarchs on their own land, until the privilege was withdrawn after the '45 uprising.

In 1766 Sir James Grant , in an attempt to medernize Grant lands and prevent the break-up of the clan, built the completely new town of Grantown-on-Spey, complete with mills and factories.

GRANT OF MONYMUSK *A variant of this pattern, dated 1816, can be found in the Cockburn Collection, Glasgow.*

The clan has strong American associations. One of the most colourful members of the Ballindalloch line was General James Grant. After serving as a profess-ional soldier in Austria and the Low Countries, he arrived in America during the War of Independence. There, he was closely involved in the capture of Havana and St. Lucia, before becoming Governor of East Florida. In the following century, General Ulysses S. Grant (1822–1885) led the Union forces during the American Civil War (1861–1865) before becoming the 18th US President.

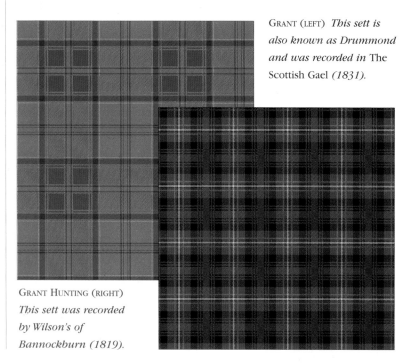

GRANT (LEFT) *This sett is also known as Drummond and was recorded in* The Scottish Gael *(1831).*

GRANT HUNTING (RIGHT) *This sett was recorded by Wilson's of Bannockburn (1819).*

BALLINDALLOCH CASTLE *Dating from 1546, this has long been the home of the Grants or the Macpherson Grants. From here, the family engaged in a lengthy feud with the Grants of Casson.*

Graham

ACCORDING TO A picturesque legend, the ancestor of this clan was a Caledonian warrior named Gramus, who led his men in a daring raid across the Antonine Wall. To commemorate this, part of the wall was dubbed 'Graeme's Dyke'. More prosaically, the name probably came from the Norman manor of Gregham ('Grey home'), which was cited in the Domesday Book. The family travelled north after the accession of David I, when William de Graham was granted the lands of Dalkeith and Abercorn by the new king.

The clan is popularly known as 'the Gallant Grahams', a nickname earned by their prowess in battle. Sir John de Graham, fought alongside William Wallace and became known as 'Graham of the Bright Sword'. He perished at the Battle of Falkirk in 1298.

The most famous of Graham military leaders was James Graham, 5th Earl and 1st Marquis of Montrose (1612–1650). Although he opposed the religious policies of Charles I, his political sympathies lay with the Royalists, and at the outbreak of the Civil War he offered his services to the king. Charles made him his Lieutenant-General and Montrose took command of a mixed force of Highlanders, Islanders, and Irishmen, including Alasdair MacDonald, the infamous 'Colkitto'.

Montrose's army was undisciplined and, at times, quite brutal. Nevertheless, they cut a swathe through Parliament's forces in Scotland. In September 1644, they routed Lord Elcho at Tippermuir, and captured Perth and Aberdeen. They

trounced the Campbells, before winning another victory at Inverlochy. Dundee fell in April 1645 and, after further successes at Auldearn and Kilsyth, the Lowlands seemed ready to fall. These hopes foundered when the Royalists suffered a crushing defeat at Philiphaugh. Montrose disbanded the remnants of his army and escaped to Norway.

After the execution of Charles I (1649), Montrose made an ill-judged attempt to restore the monarchy. His tiny army was dispersed at Carbisdale (1650) and he was betrayed to his enemies by MacLeod of Assynt. Taken to Edinburgh, he was hanged and quartered.

John Graham of Claverhouse, Viscount Dundee (1649–1689), also gave his life for the Stuart cause. He served in the army of William of Orange, but was bitterly opposed to the 'Glorious Revolution' of 1688, when the Dutchman replaced James VII on the throne. Graham threatened to reverse the situation, after winning a resounding victory at Killiecrankie (1689), but he was killed during the fighting.

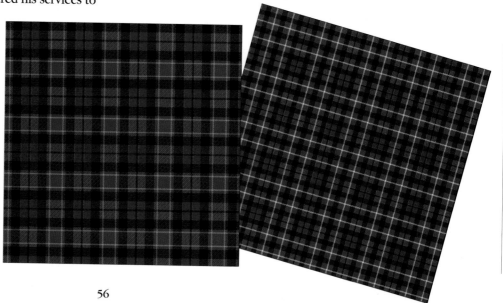

GRAHAM OF MENTEITH (RIGHT) *This pattern is from Logan's book* The Scottish Gael *(1831), although an older sample has survived (1816).*

GRAHAM OF MONTROSE (FAR RIGHT) *There is a verified sample of this tartan in the Cockburn Collection (1815).*

Gunn

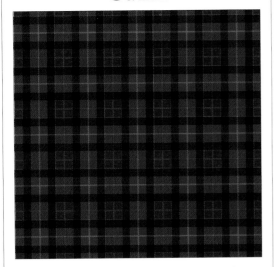

This sett was recorded by James Logan in
The Scottish Gael *(1831).*

Aⁿ WARLIKE CLAN from the far north, their name, is derived from the Norse word *gunnr* ('war'). The Gunns were based in Sutherland and Caithness, claiming descent from Olaf the Black, the Norse King of the Isle of Man. Throughout their early history, they conducted a bitter feud with the Keiths, culminating in the Battle of Harpsdale (1426). An attempted reconciliation at the Chapel of St Tears went awry, when George Gunn was ambushed and killed (1464). After this, the Gunns declined. They were listed among the 'broken clans' in 1594 and suffered badly in the Clearances. Many of these problems were described in the novels of Neil Gunn (1891-1973).

Guthrie

Named after the Barony of Guthrie, this clan is based in Angus, inland of Arbroath.

ALTHOUGH THE DERIVATION of the name is uncertain, it has been suggested that it comes from Guthrum, a Viking chief. In any event, it was first documented in 1178, when William the Lion presented the estates of Gutherin to Arbroath Abbey. Soon after, the land was purchased by a royal falconer and, in 1299, the Laird of Guthrie was sent to France, to escort Sir William Wallace back to his native land. The Guthries remained loyal servants of the Crown, most notably Sir David Guthrie, who held the posts of royal armour bearer, Lord Treasurer and Lord Chief Justice. He also built Guthrie Castle (1468), which was the family seat until the present century.

Haig

A regimental tartan of 1908, adopted by Earl Haig's family.

PETRUS DE HAGA, a Norman lord and founder of the clan, was cited as a witness on several 12th-century charters. These described him as 'Dominus de Bemersyde' ('Master of Bemersyde'), a stronghold near Dryburgh. The association between family and property was well known, as a prophecy by Thomas the Rhymer confirms: 'Tide, tide, whate'er betide; There'll aye be Haigs at Bemersyde'. The Haigs distinguished themselves as soldiers. The most famous of all was Earl Haig, the Commander-in-Chief of British forces during World War I. In recognition of his services, Bemersyde was purchased for him by public subscription, so that the Rhymer's prophecy could be fulfilled.

Hamilton

Probably designed by Allan Hay for the
Vestiarium Scoticum *(1842).*

THE NAME STEMS from the town of Hambleton in northern England. In Scotland, it was first linked with a Norman lord, Walter Fitz Gilbert of Hameldone, who witnessed a charter about fishing rights in 1294. He owned land in Renfrewshire, but was later presented with estates in Lanarkshire by Robert the Bruce, including Cadzow, now the town of Hamilton. The family rose to a great height, acquiring many titles, such as the Earl of Arran (1503), the Earl of Abercorn (1603), and the Duke of Hamilton (1643). Often, they were heirs presumptive to the Scottish throne. The family owned many splendid properties, most notably Hamilton Palace, which was demolished in 1927.

Hannay

Based on a kilt worn by Commander
Alex Hannay (1788-1844).

HAILING FROM THE ancient region of Galloway, the Hannays came from Celtic roots. Early records confirm their opposition to Robert the Bruce. Gilbert de Hannethes signed the Ragman Rolls in 1296, and his kinsmen openly supported John Balliol's quest for power. Gradually, the family increased its standing, erecting Sorbie Tower (*c.*1550) on their lands. This remained their ancestral seat until the clan was outlawed in the 17th century, following a disastrous feud with the Murrays. At this stage, many of the Hannays fled to Ulster, where the name is still very common. In later years, the Hannays of Kirkdale became the principal branch of the family.

Hay

This pattern was illustrated in the Vestiarium
Scoticum, *published in 1842.*

DE HAYA, A NORMAN FAMILY, can be traced back beyond the Conquest, but its presence in Scotland dates from the 12th century, when William de Haya was cupbearer to Malcolm IV. The name stems from the De La Haye ('stockade') peninsula in Normandy. William was granted the Barony of Erroll in *c.*1172, while his younger brother was the ancestor of the Earls of Tweeddale. The family's fortunes rose still further under Robert the Bruce, who gave them Slains Castle in Aberdeenshire and the hereditary post of Lord High Constable of Scotland. The Hays were prominent activists in the two Jacobite uprisings, when the ruins of Slains Castle were used as a secret meeting place.

Henderson

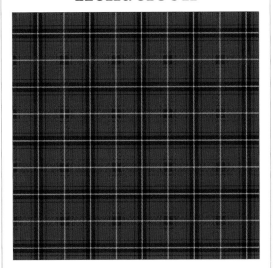

*Closely resembling the Davidson tartan, this was
first recorded by Johnston (1906).*

THE HENDERSONS ('Henry's Son') of Glencoe
claim descent from a semi-mythical Pictish
figure, 'Great Henry, Son of King Nechtan'. In
Gaelic, this is *Eanruig Mór Mac Rìgh Neachtan*
or, in its anglicized form, MacKendrick. The historical development of the clan is far from clear,
though it seems they were eventually absorbed
into the MacIains of Glencoe. The Hendersons
of Caithness sprang from a completely different
line, citing George Gunn (d.1464) as their
ancestor. In the Lowlands, meanwhile, the main
branch was the Hendersons of Fordell. Their
leading light was Alexander Henderson of
Leuchars (1583-1646), one of the chief
architects of the National Covenant (1638).

Home

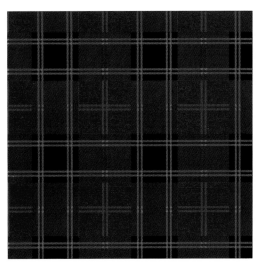

*First published in Paris in J. Claude's
Clan Originaux (1880).*

ONE OF THE greatest of the Border clans, the
Homes took their name from lands in
Berwickshire. Its literal meaning is 'cave', from
the Gaelic word *uamh*. Aldan de Home was the
first recorded ancestor (1170s), while William
de Home featured in a number of 13th-century
documents relating to Coldstream Monastery.
His descendant, Alexander, was made Lord
Home in 1473 and the title of earl was acquired
in 1603. The best-known family members are
David Hume (1711-1776), the distinguished
philosopher, and Sir Alec Douglas Home, who
renounced his peerage to become UK Prime
Minister in 1963. On his return to the House of
Lords, he took the title Lord Home of the Hirsel.

Hope

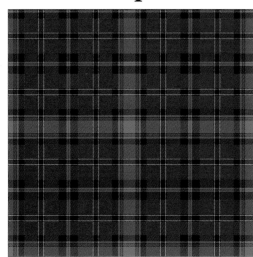

*A sample of this tartan was deposited with the
Highland Society of London in c.1815.*

ALTHOUGH A JOHN DE HOP of Peeblesshire was
listed in the Ragman Rolls (1296), the line
can only be traced back with certainty to John
de Hope, who arrived in Scotland in 1537 with
Princess Madeleine, James V's French bride.
Hope's grandson, Sir Thomas, had a distinguished
career as Lord Advocate and was made a baronet
in 1628. His successor assumed the title of Lord
Craighall, after his estates in Fifeshire. The
Hopetoun branch of the family stemmed from
Sir Thomas's younger son. They gained the titles
of Earl of Hopetoun (1703) and Marquess of
Linlithgow (1902), and their ancestral home,
Hopetoun House, is one of the greatest
architectural masterpieces in Scotland.

Hunter

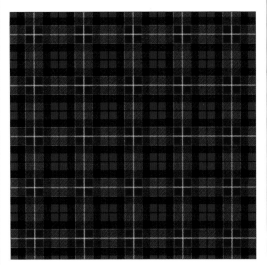

*Also known as Galbraith and Russell,
this Hunter pattern dates from 1819.*

THE HUNTERS COME from Norman stock. According to tradition, one of their ancestors fought with Rollo at the sack of Paris (896), while others became official huntsmen to the Dukes of Normandy. The family crossed the Channel after the Conquest, settling in Scotland during the reign of David I (1124-1153). They were granted the lands of Hunter's Toune – now Hunterston – in Ayrshire. The family has distinguished itself on the battlefield. John, 14th Laird, fought and died at Flodden (1513); and Lt. General Sir Aylmer Hunter-Weston was involved in the Boer War and the Gallipoli landings (1915).

Inglis

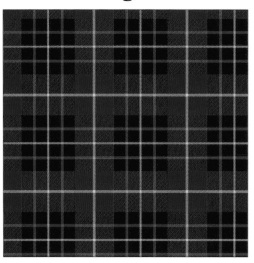

*This is a variant of the MacIntyre tartan, from
James MacKinlay's collection (c.1930-1950).*

INGLIS MEANS 'Englishman', applied equally to those who fled north after the Conquest and to later Anglo-Norman adventurers. In the earliest known document (c.1153), Richard Anglicus witnessed a royal charter granted to Melrose Abbey. At the end of the 14th century, Sir William Inglis gained fame as a swordsman, defeating the English champion in single combat and gaining the Barony of Manner as his reward. This branch of the family was closely allied to the Clan Douglas. In time, the Inglises of Cramond gained the ascendancy. Now a suburb of Edinburgh, these lands were purchased in 1624 and James Inglis of Cramond was made a baronet in 1687.

Innes

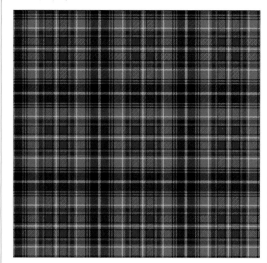

*A modern tartan, this was approved by
Lord Lyon, King of Arms, in 1938.*

THE CLAN TAKES its name from the Barony of Innes (literally 'greens') in Moray. In 1160, these lands were granted to Berowald of Flanders by Malcolm IV. His grandson adopted the name in 1226. In the 14th century, the family estates were enlarged, following the marriage of Sir Alexander, 9th of that ilk, to the daughter of the Thane of Aberchirder. The title of Baronet was added in 1625 and Sir James, 6th Baronet, succeeded as the 5th Duke of Roxburgh in 1805. Notable family members have included John Innes, Bishop of Moray, who rebuilt Elgin Cathedral after its destruction by the Wolf of Badenoch (1390), and Cosmo Innes (1793-1874), the historian.

Irvine

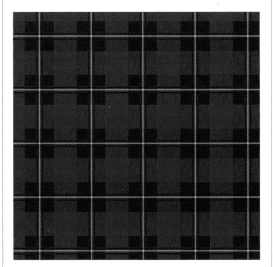

The design of this Lowland tartan is thought to date back to c.1889.

Irvine probably derives from the old English Christian name of Erewine or Erwinne. By the Middle Ages, it had also become a place name, attached to lands in Dumfriesshire and Ayrshire. The earliest family member of note was William de Irwin, who lived at Lochmaben and was a trusty supporter of Robert the Bruce. He served as the king's armour bearer and clerk and, in 1324, Bruce rewarded him with the Forest of Drum, in Aberdeenshire. This contained an imposing 13th-century tower and, over the centuries, the Irvines added to it, transforming it into one of the finest castles in the country. It remained the family seat until 1976, when it was taken over by the National Trust.

Jardine

The tartan of one of the Border clans, based at Applegirth in Dumfriesshire.

The clan has Norman roots, taking its name from the French word for 'garden' (*jardin*). The family arrived in Britain with William the Conqueror, settling in Scotland in the first half of the 12th century. In 1178, Humphrey de Jardin witnessed a charter relating to Arbroath Abbey and, some 30 years later, Patrick de Gardinus was appointed chaplain to the Bishop of Glasgow. By the 14th century, the Jardines were established at Applegirth, on the shores of the River Annan, and this has remained their principal seat. Many of the family distinguished themselves overseas, most notably Dr William Jardine, who became a co-founder of the Jardine Matheson trading house in Hong Kong (1827).

Johnstone

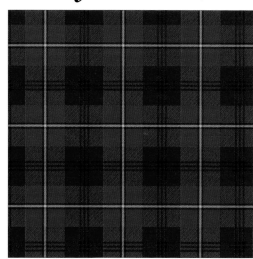

A sample of this tartan was included in Paton's collection, dating from the 1830s.

A powerful border clan, taking its name from the Barony of Johnstone in Annandale. Sir Gilbert de Johnstoun and his immediate heirs figured in a number of 13th-century documents, but there is little detailed information before 1448, when Adam Johnstone is known to have fought in the Battle of Sark. The clan was much feared in northern England, because of its frequent raids across the border, and it also became embroiled in a long-running feud against the Maxwells. James Johnstone was made a Lord in 1633 and, a decade later, was created Earl of Hartfell. Later in the century, the extinct Earldom of Annandale was added to the family's titles.

Keith

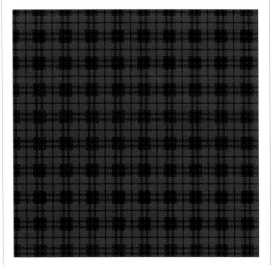

*The Keith or Austin tartan was first recorded
by Wilson's of Bannockburn (1819).*

THE KEITH'S first documented ancestor was a
Norman named Hervey who received the
lands of Keth, in Lothian, in *c*.1150. Hervey's
son was appointed Great Marischal of Scotland
in 1176, responsible for the safety of both the
king and the Scottish regalia. The post remained
in the family until the 18th century. Sir William
Keith was created Earl Marischal in 1458 and
his descendant, George, 4th Earl, founded
Aberdeen's Marischal College in 1593.

DUNNOTTAR CASTLE *During the Civil War, the
Honours of Scotland (the regalia) were concealed
in this Keith stronghold.*

KENNEDY SEE PAGE **64**

Kerr

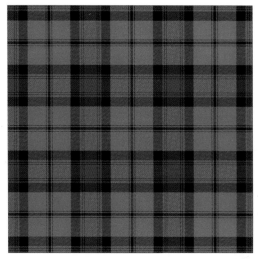

*The Kerr tartan was first described in
the* Vestiarium Scoticum *(1842).*

THE ORIGINS OF the name are disputed,
although the Norse word *kjrr* ('marsh
dweller') and the Gaelic *caer* ('fortress') are
both possibilities. By tradition, however, the
founders of the clan were Anglo-Norman: two
brothers named Ralph and John, who settled in
Roxburgh in *c*.1330. From this pair sprang rival
branches of the clan, the Kerrs of Ferniehurst
and the Kerrs of Cessford. They chose different
sides in virtually every political cause until
1631, when they were finally reconciled by
the marriage of William Kerr of Ferniehurst to
the Cessford heiress. Both sides of the highly
influential family, at different times, held the
important post of Warden of the Middle March.

Kennedy

THE CLAN NAME probably derives from the Gaelic word *Ceannaideach* ('Ugly Head'), the somewhat blunt nickname of Roland, one of the earliest Kennedys. The family claim descent from a 12th-century nobleman, Duncan, 1st Earl of Carrick, but their lineage comes into sharp focus only in c.1360, when John Kennedy of Dunure acquired the lands of Cassillis. He had already forged a link with the Ayrshire Earls through his marriage to Mary de Carrick.

The Kennedys rose to prominence in the following century, when John's grandson, James, married Princess Mary, one of the daughters of

KENNEDY (BELOW RIGHT) *This sett is undated, but a sample was featured in Paton's collection, which was assembled in the 1830s.*

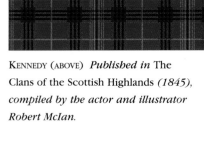

KENNEDY (ABOVE) *Published in* The Clans of the Scottish Highlands *(1845), compiled by the actor and illustrator Robert McIan.*

Robert III. Their son, Gilbert, was created Lord Kennedy in 1457 and was later appointed to the council of regents, who governed Scotland during the minority of James III. Gilbert's brother, James, also had a distinguished career, serving briefly as Lord High Chancellor. He subsequently became Archbishop of St Andrews, where he founded St Salvator's College (1455).

In 1509, Sir David, 3rd Lord Kennedy, was made Earl of Cassillis. He enjoyed the honour for only a short time, as he was among the flower of the Scottish nobility who fell at Flodden (1513). His successors fared little better, for Gilbert, 2nd Earl, was assassinated by Sir Hugh Campbell in 1527, while the 3rd Earl was poisoned at Dieppe. John, 4th Earl, brought the name of the clan into disrepute. In 1570, he abducted the Abbot of Crossraguel and took him to his castle at Dunure. There, it is said, he roasted the unfortunate cleric in soap, in an attempt to make him sign away the abbey lands. His motive, perhaps, was that Crossraguel had been endowed by his ancestor, Duncan, Earl of Carrick (1244).

The 8th Earl died without heirs and there was a three-year court dispute, before the succession was settled on Sir Thomas Kennedy of Culzean. He set about improving the family estates and his brother, the 10th Earl, continued his work, commissioning Robert Adam to transform Culzean Castle into one of the most beautfiul houses in Scotland.

On the death of the 10th Earl, the title passed to Captain Archibald Kennedy, a former naval officer who had made his fortune in America and who lived at No.1, Broadway, New York. He tried to remain neutral during the War of Independence but, even so, his Broadway home was confiscated by Washington. The 12th Earl was a close friend of William IV and was given a new honour – the title of Marquess of Ailsa – at the time of his coronation (1831).

Kilgour

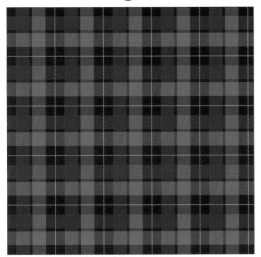

*A copy of this design was lodged with the
Scottish Tartans Society in the 1980s.*

THE KILGOURS have very strong associations
with Fife. They took their name from the
lands of Kilgour, near Falkland, and were
followers of the MacDuffs, the Earls of Fife.
Before it became a royal palace, Falkland was a
MacDuff stronghold and it is probably no
accident that the earliest reference to a Kilgour
relates to this place. For, in 1528, Sir Thomas
Kilgour was cited as chaplain of St Thomas at
Falkland. He may well be the Thomas Kingoure,
who was mentioned in 1567 in connection
with a pension of forty-five shillings. Many
Kilgours emigrated to northern Australia, where
there is a river bearing this name.

Kincaid

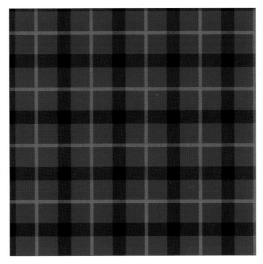

*This sett was in the MacGregor-Hastie Collection
and probably dates from c.1930-1950.*

OF TERRITORIAL ORIGIN, the clan name describes
the land between the River Kelvin and the
River Glazert, and the word itself may come
from the Gaelic *ceann cadha* ('steep place'). As
a family, the Kincaids were comparative late-
comers, for the property was initially held by
the Earls of Lennox and the Galbraiths.
However, they took it over in the late 13th
century, subsequently adding Craiglockhart and
Blackness Castle to their possessions. The latter
was an important stronghold, used in the 17th
century as a prison for Covenanters. The
Kincaids fought on the losing side in the Civil
War and the Jacobite uprisings and, as a result,
many of them emigrated to the New World.

Kinnieson

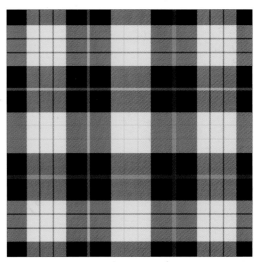

*This pattern was recorded in the
MacGregor-Hastie Collection (c.1930-1950).*

A RECOGNIZED SEPT of the MacFarlanes, the
family name is thought to be a variant of
Cunieson, which means 'Son of Conan'. The
name is most common in Atholl, where it may
stem from Conan de Glenerochy, the illegitimate son of Henry, Earl of Atholl. It is found in
many 15th- and 16th-century documents. In
1474, for example, John Cunyson held the lands
of Ardgery, in the Barony of Eddradoun.
Similarly, in the following century, the
Chronicle of Fortirgall recorded the death of
Johannis Cwnyson de Edderdedowar.

Lamont

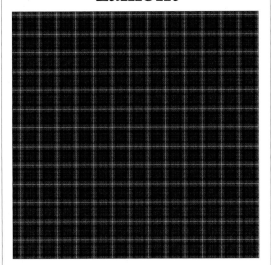

Dating from c.1810, this is similar to the tartan worn by the Campbells of Argyll.

THE NAME IS taken from the ancient Norse word for 'lawman' (*logmaor*). Originally, the family came from Ulster, perhaps from the line of the O'Neills of Tyrone. Their arrival in Scotland can be traced back to *c*.1200, when Ferchar became the founder of the clan. His grandson, Laumun, was the first to bear the family name and, in 1456, John Lamond was cited as the baillie of Cowal. Increasingly, the clan became a force in the West, basing their strength on the castles of Toward, near Dunoon, and Ascog, on the Isle of Bute. Their power evaporated after 1646, however, when 200 clansmen were massacred by the Campbells and their strongholds were destroyed.

Lauder

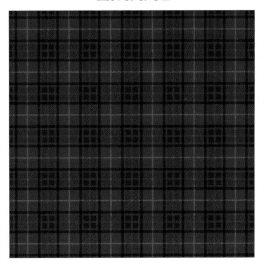

This may have been designed by Sir Thomas Lauder for the Sobieskis' book (1842).

ORIGINALLY A NORMAN family, the Lauders settled in Scotland during the reign of Malcolm Canmore (1058-1093). Sir Robert de Lawedre was a supporter of both Wallace and Robert the Bruce, serving the latter as an ambassador. In the 15th century, William Lauder rose to become Bishop of Glasgow and Chancellor of Scotland. In recent times, the name has been closely associated with the Music Hall star, Sir Harry Lauder (1870-1950), but his real name was Hugh MacLennan.

BASS ROCK *For a time, the Lauders owned this tiny island with its mighty castle. A strategic stronghold, it was also used as a prison for Covenanters.*

Leask

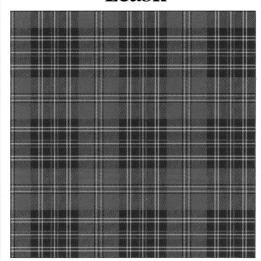

This tartan was designed by Madam Leask and approved in 1981.

ALTHOUGH THE SOURCE of the name is not certain, Liscus, a Gaulish chieftain, and the Norman family of de Lesque have both been mooted as possible ancestors. Even so, there is no record of the clan in Scotland until 1296, when William de Laskereske put his name to one of the Ragman Rolls. In *c*.1345, William Leask received confirmation of his lands at Leskgaranne and, in the following century, another member of the clan settled in Orkney, founding a new branch of the family. The family fortunes nosedived in the 18th century, when Alexander Leask was bankrupted after speculating in the Darien scheme, an unsuccessful trading venture in Panama.

Lennox

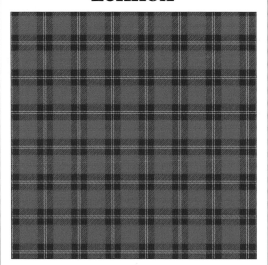

This tartan featured in a 16th-century portrait of the Countess of Lennox.

THE NAME OF Lennox is attached to a powerful earldom, controlling large tracts of Dunbartonshire, Renfrewshire, and Stirlingshire. It evolved from an ancient Celtic title, the Mormaer of Levenach ('smooth stream'), and was firmly established by the 13th century. Malcolm, 5th Earl, was one of Bruce's supporters and his son attended the coronation of Robert II (1371). After 1488, the title became associated with the Stewarts and, more particularly, the Darnleys. Henry, Lord Darnley – the short-lived husband of Mary Queen of Scots - was the son of the 4th Stewart Earl. Esmé Stuart was created Duke of Lennox in 1579, becoming High Chamberlain of Scotland two years later.

Leslie

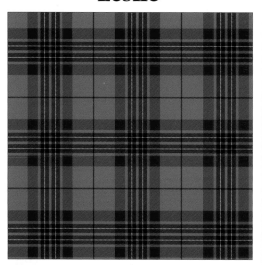

This dress tartan dates from 1842, but the Leslie hunting tartan is older.

ORIGINATING FROM the Barony of Leslie, in the Garioch district of Aberdeenshire, the first to assume the name was Bartholf, a Hungarian nobleman who was appointed Governor of Edinburgh Castle by Malcolm III. Alexander Leslie, Earl of Leven (1580-1661) served under Gustavus Adolphus, before returning to command the Covenanters' army (1638), while Walter, Count Leslie (1606-1667) fought in the Austrian army and was involved in the assassination of Wallenstein.

PITCAPLE CASTLE *In c.1457, David Leslie, 1st Baron of Pitcaple, began the castle, which remained in family hands until 1757.*

Lindsay

Featured in The Clans of the Highlands of Scotland *by T. Smibert (1850).*

THE LINDSAYS WERE an Anglo-Norman family and the surname derives from their original estate ('the island of the lime tree'). They settled in Scotland in the 12th century, when Sir Walter de Lindissie joined the Council of Prince David. His descendant, Sir William, became Baron of Luffness, while Sir David was created Earl of Crawford in 1398. The Lindsays of Balcarres and the Lindsays of Edzell were important, secondary branches of the family. The former were descended from the 9th Earl of Crawford and became earls in their own right in 1650. The latter built the superb Renaissance castle of Edzell, near Brechin.

Livingstone

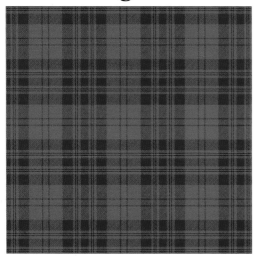

This is a modern tartan, resembling the sett of the Stewarts of Appin.

APPARENTLY, THE name derives from a Saxon lord called Leving, who held the lands of Levingstoun in West Lothian during Edgar's reign (1097-1107). Sir William Livingston campaigned with David II in England and was captured at the Battle of Durham (1346). He was rewarded with the Barony of Callendar. The Livingstons of Argyll were a separate branch, claiming descent from a physician to the Lord of the Isles. They were a small clan, based on the Isle of Lismore, and they were closely linked with the Stewarts of Appin. Their most famous family member was Dr David Livingstone (1813-1873), the explorer and missionary.

Lockhart

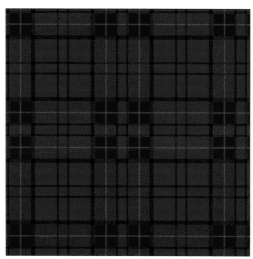

The tartan of a Lowland clan, most prominent in Lanarkshire and Ayrshire.

THE LOCARDS WERE one of many families displaced from their English lands by the Norman Conquest. By the 12th century, they had settled at Lee in Lanarkshire. There is a romantic tale concerning Sir Simon Locard, one of the Scots who carried Robert the Bruce's heart on a crusade in 1329. Simon was entrusted with the key to this precious casket and, to commemorate this, he changed his name to Lockheart. The crusade proved a failure but, before it was aborted, Simon acquired a mystical charm, a stone with supposed healing powers. This became known as the Lee Penny, and Scott used it as the basis for his novel, *The Talisman* (1825).

Logan

This is one of several Logan tartans, produced by Wilson's of Bannockburn (1819).

THERE ARE TWO distinct branches of the Logan clan, a Highland and a Lowland one. The latter dates back to at least the 14th century. Sir Robert and Sir Walter Logan both joined the force which carried Bruce's heart on a crusade, losing their lives in Spain (1329). Then, in 1400, another Sir Robert gained the post of Lord High Admiral. The Logans of the North were also known as the MacLennans. They stemmed from Crotair MacGilligorm, a hunchbacked member of the Logans of Drumderfit. He went into orders, married, and named his son after Saint Finnan. This was the origin of the MacLennans, for the Gaelic version of their name means 'Son of Finnan's Servant'.

Lumsden

This tartan belongs to the Lumsdens, a Border clan, hailing from Berwickshire.

O F TERRITORIAL ORIGIN, the name derives from lands near Coldingham in Berwickshire. These were first mentioned in 1098, when King Edgar granted the manor of Lumsdene to Coldingham Priory. Both Gillem and Cren de Lummisden were owners of the property in the mid-12th century, but the recognized founder of the clan was Adam de Lumisden of that ilk, whose name appears on the Ragman Rolls (1296). Gilbert Lumsden then acquired the lands of Blanerne through marriage (1329). Notable members of the clan included Sir James Lumsden, who fought for Gustavus Adolphus in the Thirty Years' War, and Andrew Lumsden, who was secretary to the Old Pretender in Rome.

MacAlister

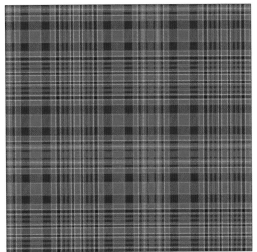

This design was first illustrated in W. & A. Smith's Authenticated Tartans *(1850).*

T HIS FAMILY WAS an offshoot of the great Clan Donald. Their name means 'Son of Alastair', the ancestor in question being Alastair Mor, son of Donald, Lord of the Isles. The MacAlisters are well documented from 1366, when Ranald, son of Alexander, was cited as chief of the clan. At this stage, the family lands were mainly in Kintyre, but they also gained considerable possessions on the islands of Bute and Arran. By the end of the 15th century, the main branch were the MacAlisters of Loup, so-called because the boundary of their territory took the form of a bend in the river (in Gaelic, a *lub*).

MacAlpine

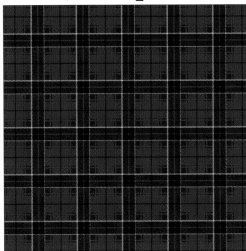

First recorded in W. & A.K. Johnston's The Tartans of the Clans and Septs of Scotland *(1906).*

M ACALPINE ANCESTRY is very distinguished. The founder of the clan was Alpin, a 9th-century king of Dalriada, reputedly slain by the Picts in 834. His son, Kenneth MacAlpin was much more famous. In *c.*843, he managed to unite the thrones of Dalriada and the Picts, thereby forming the nucleus of the future Scottish nation. The later history of the *Siol Alpine* ('Race of Alpin') is much less clear, as it includes many other clans. The most illustrious family members were John MacAlpyn, better known as Machabeus (d.1557), an ardent religious reformer, and Sir Robert McAlpine, the founder of a successful firm of civil engineers.

MacArthur

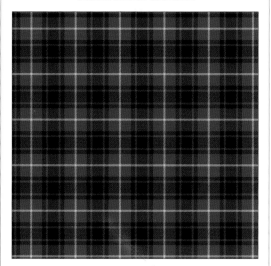

*Based on a MacDonald tartan, this was
first recorded in 1842.*

ACCORDING TO A popular proverb, 'There is nothing older, unless the hills, MacArthur, and the devil'. The MacArthurs began as a branch of the Campbells and were loyal supporters of Robert the Bruce. He rewarded them with the lands of his enemies, the MacDougalls. The clan remained a powerful force until 1427, when the Chief was executed by James I. More recent prominent figures include General Douglas MacArthur (1880-1964).

DUNSTAFFNAGE CASTLE *In the mid-15th century, the Chief of the MacArthurs was made Captain of this Argyllshire Castle.*

MacAulay

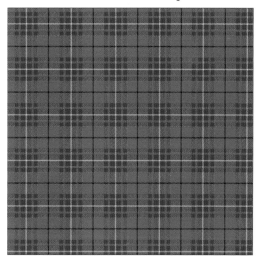

*First published in 1881, this pattern has also
been linked with the Comyns.*

THERE ARE TWO unconnected MacAulay lines. The MacAulays ('Sons of Olaf') of Lewis claim descent from Olaf the Black. They held land in Ross and Sutherland, later becoming followers of the MacLeods of Lewis. Their most famous son was Thomas Babington, 1st Lord MacAulay (1800-1859), the statesman, essayist, and historian. The other family are the MacAulays of Ardincaple, in Dunbartonshire, who are closely linked with the Lennox clan. Their ancestor was Aulay, brother to the Earl of Lennox, and they were confirmed as vassals of the clan in a roll of Highland landlords (1587). The lands of Ardincaple were eventually sold to the Duke of Argyll in 1767.

MacBain

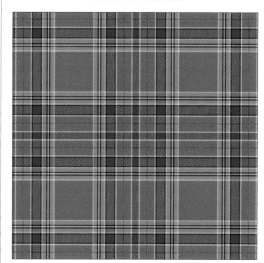

*This 1847 variation of the MacBain tartan is
based on Robert McIan's earlier design.*

THE NAME COMES in several forms, including MacBain, MacBean, and MacVean. All claim as their ancestor Donald Ban, the Scottish king (ruled 1093-1097), featured in Shakespeare's *Macbeth*. The family belonged to the Clan Chattan, an ancient confederation of clans, and they were also known as supporters of Robert the Bruce. One of their number was credited with killing the steward of Red Comyn, Bruce's deadly rival. The main branch of the family were the MacBeans of Kinchyle, on Loch Ness, where there is now a MacBain Memorial Park. The clan's greatest figure was William MacBean, who won the Victoria Cross in 1858 for his bravery during the Indian Mutiny.

MacBeth

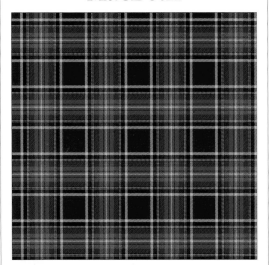

The traditional tartan of this Morayshire clan is also known as the Blue Stewart.

THE NAME of this clan will always carry over-tones of Shakespeare's tragic Scottish king. The real Macbeth (ruled 1040-1057) had little in common with the villainous figure portrayed in the play. He had a valid claim to the throne and slew his rival on the battlefield, not in the bedchamber. He is said to have ruled wisely and generously, finding time to make a pilgrimage to Rome, where he 'scattered money among the poor like seed'. The MacBeths of Moray were the principal branch of the clan, while the Bethunes and Beatons were secondary off-shoots. The latter were hereditary physicians to the MacDonalds of Islay.

MacCallum

Recorded in D. W. Stewart's Old and Rare Scottish Tartans, published in 1893.

A NAME OF ECCLESIASTICAL character, it means a follower of Columba (c.521-597), the Iona-based saint and missionary who converted much of Scotland. There is also a tradition that the clan originated from the district of Lorn, in Argyllshire, where three brothers founded the main branches of the family – the MacCallums of Colgin, Glen Etive, and Kilmartin. In 1414, the chief was made hereditary Constable of the Castles of Craignish and Lochaffy. Then, in later years, there were growing links with the Malcolm clan. These appear to date from c.1779, when Dugald MacCallum changed his name to Malcolm, shortly after inheriting the estate of Poltalloch.

MacColl

Originally known as Old Bruce, this tartan was produced by Wilson's (1797).

TRADITIONALLY ACCEPTED as a branch of the Clan Donald, the MacColls have long been associated with the area around Loch Fyne. Details of their early history are sketchy, although it is known that they became involved in a feud with the Macphersons. This resulted in a bloody skirmish at Drum Nachder in 1602, when the MacColls were roundly defeated. More recently, the name has acquired artistic associations. Evan McColl (1808-1898) was a noted Gaelic poet, the author of *The Mountain Minstrel*, while Ewan MacColl (1915-1989) made his mark as a folk-singer, the winner of both a Grammy and an Ivor Novello Award.

MacDiarmid

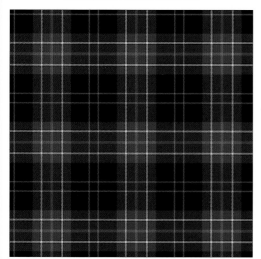

First published in Johnston's The Tartans of the Clans and Septs of Scotland *(1906).*

THIS ANCIENT family is a recognized sept of the Campbells. Their name means 'Son of Dermid' or 'Dermot' and is spelled in a bewildering variety of ways. The MacDiarmids of Glenlyon claim to be the oldest branch. In 1427, Nemeas Mactarmayt was the rector of St Conganus de Duybrinis (Durinish), later becoming vicar of Kilchoman in Islay. In 1502, John Makeyrmit was listed as a victim of the hership ('plundering') of Petty, while Jhone McChormeit of Menyenis signed a legal bond in 1533. Colin MacDermot, the bard of Reay, was drowned in 1799.

MacDONALD SEE PAGES 76–77,
MacDONELL SEE PAGES 78–79

MacDougall

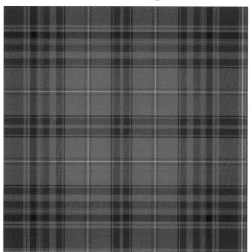

The oldest surviving sample of a MacDougall tartan dates from c.1815-1816.

THE CLAN IS descended from Dugall, eldest son of Somerled, Lord of the Isles. His successor, Duncan, held Lorn and many of the Western Isles, including Jura, Mull, and Lismore. This meant that the MacDougalls had divided loyalties until 1263, when Haakon's invasion forced them to choose between Norway and Scotland. Their relationship with the Comyns led them to oppose Robert the Bruce and, accordingly, he seized many of their lands. This damage was repaired in 1354, when Ewen MacDougall married Bruce's granddaughter. In later years, the clan was staunchly loyal to the Stuarts, supporting Charles in the Civil War and participating in the first Jacobite rebellion.

MacDuff

The regimental weavers, Wilson's of Bannockburn, used this pattern in 1819.

FROM EARLY TIMES, the MacDuffs held the title of the Earl of Fife. There is a popular tradition that the 1st Earl was synonomous with the character in Shakespeare's *Macbeth*, who helped depose the usurper and place Malcolm on the throne. Despite this, the first recorded earl was Ethelred, one of Malcolm's sons, who later became the Abbot of Dunkeld. The MacDuffs enjoyed a number of special privileges, as defined in an Act of 1384: they had the honour of leading the king to his throne on coronation day; the right to lead the royal army; and the right of sanctuary at the cross of MacDuff, near Newburgh.

MacDonald

THE MACDONALDS WERE the largest and most influential of all the Highland clans. At one time, they held sway over most of western Scotland, with further possessions in Ireland and the Isle of Man. Control of this northern empire was maintained by nine independent branches of the clan which, between them, produced at least twenty-seven different tartans.

There are various interpretations of the origins of the MacDonalds. Some genealogists claimed that their line could be traced right back to Conn of the Hundred Battles, a semi-mythical high king of Ireland, who was said to have ruled in the 2nd century AD. Conn's descen-

dants, the sons of Colla, were hailed as the first settlers in the Hebrides, eventually becoming known as the Clan Cholla – the ancestors of the MacDonalds.

In more certain historical terms, the clan stemmed from the 12th-century dynasty of Somerled, King of the Isles. He regarded himself as an independent ruler, owing greater allegiance to Norway than to Scotland, and he died doing battle with Malcolm IV. The MacDonalds took their name from his grandson, Donald of Islay, who maintained this independent stance. During the next century, how-ever, the position became more complicated. The Norse influ-

FLORA MACDONALD *It was Flora who helped Bonnie Prince Charlie escape to Skye by disguising him as her Irish maid.*

ence began to wane, following their defeat at Largs in 1263, while the rise of Wallace and Bruce created divisions within the clan. Angus Og, Donald's grandson, supported the Bruce, while Alexander, the Chief of the MacDonalds, opposed him. As a result, the latter's estates were granted to Angus, when Bruce became king.

Soon, offshoots from the main line of the MacDonalds of the Isles began to multiply. John of Islay, Angus Og's son, had two wives. His marriage, to Amy MacRury, produced three sons, the second of whom was Ranald, founder of the MacDonalds of Clanranald. Then, after his

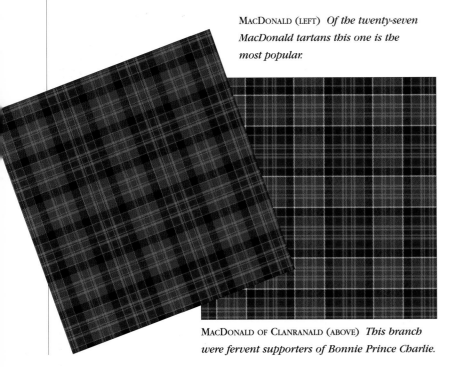

MACDONALD (LEFT) *Of the twenty-seven MacDonald tartans this one is the most popular.*

MACDONALD OF CLANRANALD (ABOVE) *This branch were fervent supporters of Bonnie Prince Charlie.*

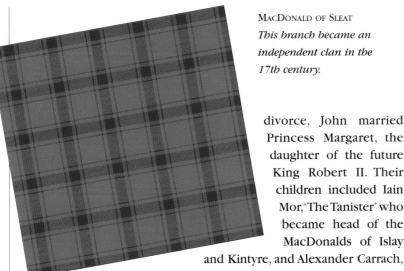

William III. The MacDonalds crossed swords with the English again, during the Jacobite Rising of 1745. Here, the greatest help came from the MacDonalds of Clanranald. Bonnie Prince Charlie raised his standard on their land and took refuge there again, after the collapse of his campaign. More famously, he received invaluable assistance from Flora MacDonald, the adopted daughter of Lady Clanranald. Flora disguised the outlawed prince as her Irish maid, Betty Burke, and helped him to escape to Skye. Despite the romantic associations of this episode, however, the rising proved a disaster for the MacDonalds, as it led to the suppression of the clan system.

divorce, John married Princess Margaret, the daughter of the future King Robert II. Their children included Iain Mor, 'The Tanister' who became head of the MacDonalds of Islay and Kintyre, and Alexander Carrach, the ancestor of the MacDonells of Keppoch.

Another branch of the family was formed when Alexander, 3rd Lord of the Isles, gave the lands of Sleat, on Skye, to his youngest son Hugh, the first MacDonald of Sleat.

For a time, it seemed as if the clan might continue to extend its influence. In 1411, Lord Donald laid claim to the earldom of Ross, which would have given him control over most of northern Scotland, but his ambitions were ended at the battle of Red Harlaw. Further uprisings took place in 1428, 1431, and 1491. The last of these was particularly serious, as it brought the MacDonalds into direct conflict with the Scottish Crown. James IV resented the fact that they had been intriguing with the English and deprived them of the Lordship of the Isles. After the Union, this title passed to the eldest son of the British monarch.

The 17th and 18th centuries saw the MacDonalds in decline. In their homelands, their power was increasingly challenged by the Campbells. This rivalry was exploited by the English in 1693, when they pressed the Campbells to massacre the MacDonalds of Glencoe, because they had been slow to swear an oath of allegiance to

CASTLE TIORAM *This 14th century stronghold belonged to the MacDonalds of Clanranald. In 1715, as he left to join the Jacobite uprising, the chief ordered it to be burned, to prevent it falling into Campbell hands.*

MacDonell

MACDONELL IS AN alternative spelling of MacDonald, used by two specific branches of the clan: the MacDonells of Glengarry and the MacDonells of Keppoch. The former share a common ancestor with the MacDonalds of Clanranald. Ranald's son, Donald, married twice. Alistair was a child of the second marriage and he became the founder of the Glengarry line.

The MacDonells did not play a signifcant role in MacDonald politics until the 16th century, when they became entangled in a series of land disputes, spanning several generations. Alexander MacDonell supported the MacDonalds in their attempts to claim the Lordship of the Isles, and was involved in the storming of Urquhart Castle (1513). In 1539, he received a royal charter for Glengarry and Morar, along with half of the estates of Lochalsh, Lochcarron, and Lochbroom. This eventually led to a bitter feud with the Mackenzies of Kintail, who owned the other half. Glengarry was taken captive and had to yield Lochcarron Castle, in order to secure his release. Then, in the early 17th century, the two clans made frequent raids into each other's territory. Kenneth Mackenzie plundered North Morar, carrying off his neighbours' cattle, while the MacDonells laid waste to Applecross and Brae Ross. Eventually, the Mackenzies managed to obtain a crown charter for the disputed land (1607).

MACDONELL OF GLENGARRY *This is the basic MacDonald sett with an additional white stripe. The oldest sample dates from 1815.*

Angus, 8th Chief of Glengarry, repaired the damage to the family fortunes by having the lands of Glengarry erected into a free barony (1627). Aeneas, his grandson and successor, fought for the Royalists during the Civil War. He was with Montrose at the Battles of Inverlochy, Auldearn, and Kilsyth (1645). Then, when the marquis was routed at Philiphaugh (1645), Aeneas gave him shelter at Invergarry Castle. He even went to the extent of leading his clan down to the Battle of Worcester (1651), where the Royalist cause foundered. At the Restoration, he was rewarded with the title of Lord MacDonell and Aros, an honour which gave him a claim to the chiefship of the

GLENGARRY *Situated in Lochaber, this MacDonell territory had formed part of the old Pictish province of Moray.*

MacDonalds. Aeneas died without a male heir, however, and the peerage became extinct (1680).

After the accession of William III, the MacDonells supported the Jacobite cause. Alexander, 11th Chief of Glengarry, took the field at Killiecrankie (1689), where he was the bearer of the Royal Standard, and was present at the Braemar hunting party, where the 1715 uprising was planned. The clan fought at Sheriffmuir and, in 1716, the Old Pretender rewarded Glengarry with the title of 'Lord MacDonell' (only recognized by the Jacobites). Alistair, 13th Chief, was imprisoned in the Tower of London during the '45 rebellion, but this did not prevent 600 of his clansmen from joining Bonnie Prince Charlie's army.

The other branch of the MacDonells, also known as Clan Ranald of Lochaber, were descended from Alistair Carrach, the third son of Ian, 7th Lord of the Isles. In common with the ancestor of the Glengarry branch, Alistair was a grandson of Robert II. He fought at the Battle of Harlaw (1411) and participated in Donald Balloch's rising in the Isles (1431). As a result, his lands were forfeited to the Crown and bestowed upon Duncan Mackintosh. This became a source of deep resentment between the two clans.

Many of the MacDonell leaders met with violent ends. The most tragic case, however, concerned the two young sons of Grey Donald, 11th Chief of Keppoch. He sent the lads away to be educated in France and, during their absence, he died.

COLONEL ALASTAIR MACDONNELL OF GLENGARRY
He formed a company from his clansmen, the Glengarry Highland Fencible Infantry, which operated from 1794 to 1801.

MACDONELL OF KEPPOCH
First published in D.W. Stewart's Old and Rare Scottish Tartans *(1893).*

They completed their training and returned in 1663, so that Alexander could assume the role of 12th Chief. Instead, they were murdered by the seven sons of their cousin, Alasdair Buidhe.

No one in the clan seemed inclined to avenge the killings, apart from Iain Lom, the Bard of Keppoch, who claimed assistance from MacDonald of Sleat. The latter provided some soldiers and, together, they tracked down the killers and beheaded them. Lom gathered up the severed heads and took them to Glengarry Castle, to lay before the chief. On the way, he stopped at a well to wash the heads. This well became known as *Tobar nan Ceann* ('the Well of the Heads'). In 1812, Alastair MacDonell commissioned a monument to be erected by the well, commemorating the act of 'ample and summary vengeance', performed by one of his ancestors.

MacEwen

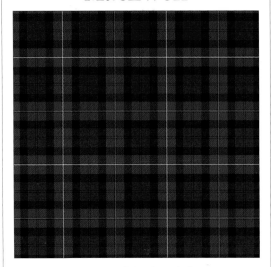

*Similar to one of the Campbell tartans,
this was first recorded in 1906.*

ALTHOUGH OF ANCIENT origin there are few authentic records of this clan. The sons of Ewen hold that they descend from Ewen of Otter, an obscure figure living in the early 13th century. His successors had a castle at Kilfinan and retained the Barony of Otter until 1432, when Swene MacEwan, 9th and last Otter Chief, granted the estates to Duncan Campbell. Without land, the MacEwans became one of the broken clans, finding their way to many districts. Some moved to Lennox territory in Dunbartonshire; others went further afield to Lochaber, Perth, Skye, and the Lowlands. The MacEwens grew strong again and made their home at Bardrochat in Ayrshire in the 17th century.

MacFadyen

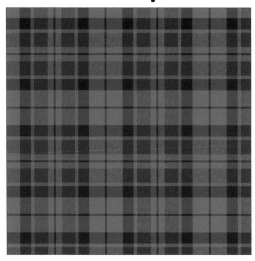

*The family that claims this tartan is associated
with the MacLaines of Lochbuie.*

MACFADYEN comes from the Gaelic *Macphaidin* ('Son of *Paidin*' or 'Little Pat'). According to an old clan tradition, the MacFadyens were the first to hold the lands of Lochbuie in Argyll. After losing them, they became a race of itinerant craftsmen. The name is first recorded in 1204, when Malcolm Macpadene witnessed a charter at Achichendone in Kintyre. Then, at the end of the century, Conghan MacPaden petitioned for the arch-deaconry of Argyll (1390). Donald Macfadzane also entered the Church, becoming a precentor at Lismore (1507) and, later, chaplain at Tibbirmore. The family was most numerous in the islands of Mull, Islay, and Tiree.

MacFarlane

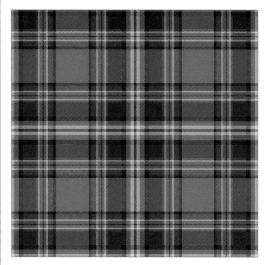

*This pattern is taken from a sash (1822) in
the Scottish Tartans Museum, Comrie.*

THE MACFARLANES claim descent from the Earls of Lennox, citing Gilchrist, the younger brother of the 3rd Earl as their ancestor. His great-grandson was called Bartholomew or, in its Gaelic form, *Parlan* (hence MacFarlane, 'Son of Parlan'). The clan was famed for its warlike behaviour. Sadly, it was also notorious for its feuds with the Colquhouns and the Buchanans. As a result, the MacFarlane name and lands were forfeited in 1642, and the clan members were dispersed.

CLADACH MOR, LOCH LOMOND *By night, clansmen used to sell stolen cattle near this spot, so locals nicknamed the moon 'MacFarlane's lantern'.*

MacFie

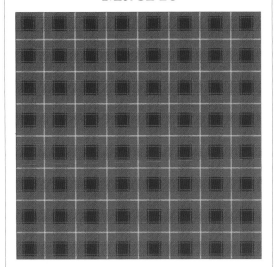

This design was first recorded in Johnston's The
Tartans of the Clans and Septs of Scotland *(1906)*

THIS CLAN LIVED on the island of Colonsay, in
the Inner Hebrides. The oldest form of the
name is MacDuffie, which appears on a charter
of 1463, but it is also written as MacFie or
MacPhee. Little information is available before
1609, when Donald Macfie of Colonsay joined
the council which drew up the Statutes of Iona,
a policy document for improving life in the
Western Isles. In 1615, Malcolm Macfie joined
the disastrous rebellion of Sir James MacDonald
of Islay. Many of the clan were killed and the
island passed to the MacDonalds. In later years,
the most notorious clansman was Ewen
Macphee, a 19th-century deserter and outlaw.

MacGill

The tartan design was included in the
MacGregor-Hastie Collection *(c.1930-1950).*

THE MACGILLS ARE associated with the
MacDonalds. Their name comes from the
Gaelic *Mac an ghoill* ('Son of the Lowlander' or
'Stranger'). The family seems to have originated
in Galloway, although it also flourished in Jura,
where the MacGills became known as the
Clann a'ghoill. In Arbroath, Maurice Macgeil
witnessed an agreement between Maldouen,
Earl of Levenach, and the church of St Thomas
the Martyr (1231). James M'Gile was a burgess
of Edinburgh in 1550, while Janet Mack Gil was
accused of being a 'disorderly person' (a non-
conformist) in 1684. Donald McGill (1875-1962)
was a noted humorist and cartoonist, best
known for his saucy seaside postcards.

MacGillivray

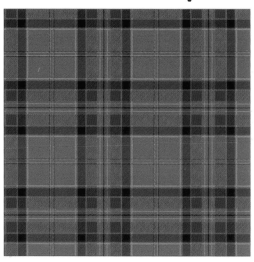

James Logan was the first to record this sett,
in The Scottish Gael *(1831).*

MACGILLIVRAY CLAN origins are uncertain.
There is a theory that it came from Mull
and took its name from Gillebride, the father of
Somerled, the 12th-century Lord of the Isles.
Other sources suggest that its roots were in
Morvern and Lochaber, and that it sought the
protection of the Mackintosh clan in 1268. In
doing so, it became one of the oldest branches
of Clan Chattan. In *c*.1500, the MacGillivrays
settled at Dunmaglass in Strathnairn, which
remained in the family until the 19th century.
The clan fought in both the Jacobite uprisings
and its chief, Alexander, died by a well at
Culloden, which still bears his name.

MACGREGOR SEE PAGES **84–85**

MacHardie

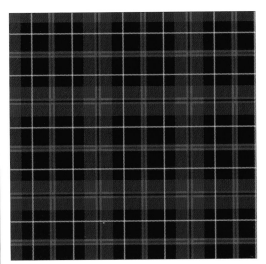

*This tartan is attributed to a sept of both the
Farquharson and Mackintosh clans.*

A HIGHLAND FAMILY, the MacHardies flourished in the Aberdeenshire region. The Strathdon branch claimed membership of the Clan Chattan Federation, acknowledging the Chief of the Mackintoses as their leader. The origin of the name is something of a mystery – the literal meaning of *Mac Chardaidh* is 'Son of the sloe'. The earliest records date from the 16th century, when Thomas McChardy was a murder victim (1560). In 1676, Donald McQhardies served as an official in the baron-bailie's court at Braemar. At around the same time, John M'Ardie and Alexander M'Kardie were listed in poll books in Invercauld.

MacIan

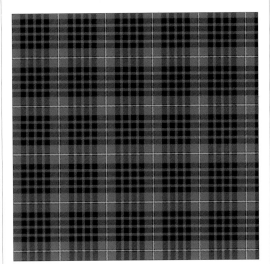

*One of the tartans recorded by the
Sobieski Stuart brothers (1842).*

THE NAME MEANS 'Son of John' and it can be found in several forms, most notably MacIain, MacKean, and MacKain. The family are connected with the Gunns, the MacDonalds of Ardnamurchan, and the MacDonalds of Glencoe. The MacIans of Ardnamurchan trace their line back to Eoin Sprangach, son of Angus Mor, a powerful Lord of the Isles in the 14th century. The MacIains of Glencoe are probably better known, for the most tragic of reasons. For Alasdair MacDonald, 12th MacIain, was the leader of the clansmen who were butchered at Glencoe (1692). He had been playing host to the Campbells, who shot him dead and gnawed his wife's fingers, to prise off her rings.

MacInnes

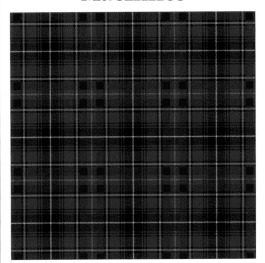

*First recorded in 1908, this design is
attributed to Onich Grocer.*

ALSO KNOWN AS the Clan Aonghais, the MacInneses ('Sons of Angus') are an ancient Celtic family. They are said to be descended from Gillebride, father of Somerled. Their traditional homelands were in the districts of Morvern and Ardnamurchan, on the Argyllshire coast. There, they are said to have become hereditary Constables of the Castle of Kinlochaline; they were still installed in the stronghold, when Coll Kitto laid siege to it in 1645. Shortly afterwards, the clan was dispersed. Some chose to follow the Campbells of Craignish, while others attached themselves to the Mackinnons. Indeed, one branch of the family became hereditary bowmen to this clan.

MacGregor

There is an old tradition that the clan is descended from Griogar, one of the sons of Kenneth MacAlpin, but this cannot be verified. Instead, it is likely that the first chief was a 14th-century figure, known as Gregor 'of the golden bridles'. Prior to this, however, the clan was firmly established in the district of Glenorchy, in Argyll. Some sources suggest that they moved there in the 11th century, but it is more probable that the lands were granted during the reign of Alexander II (1214-1249), as a reward for their assistance in the king's western campaigns. Hugh of Glenorchy was the first chief to adopt the name, followed by his kinsman, Malcolm 'the Lame', who was wounded in Ireland, fighting alongside Edward Bruce.

In the early years of the 14th century, however, the Campbells acquired a legal title to Glenorchy, a development which sowed the seeds of all the MacGregors' misfortunes. For this meant that, outside the lands of Glenstrae, which they held as vassals of the Earls of Argyll, the MacGregors were nothing more than tenants. Inevitably, a bitter feud ensued, as the Campbells tried to dislodge the clan from their territory and the MacGregors used every means to remain in their homeland.

Two events placed the clan beyond the pale. In 1589, some MacGregors killed John Drummond, a royal forester, after he had hanged some of their kinsmen for poaching. Then, in 1603, the MacGregors clashed with the Colquhouns at Glenfruin. The latter had gained a royal commission to arrest several members of the clan, for making repeated cattle raids, but Alasdair MacGregor of Glenstrae managed to trap them in a narrow glen and slaughtered them. James VI took immediate action. The Chief of the MacGregors, along with eleven of his companions, were hanged in Edinburgh. In addition, the clan was proscribed. Members of the family were obliged to adopt another surname; they were barred from meeting in groups of four or more; and they were forbidden to carry any weapon, apart from a knife with no point, which they could use for cutting their food.

These punitive measures left the MacGregors little option but to live as outlaws. As Walter Scott put it, they became 'the Children of the Mist', roaming the Highlands without a name or a home. This situation persisted throughout James' reign and the edicts were confirmed by Charles I. Despite this, members of the former clan served the Royalist cause, joining Montrose's army in 1644 and the Earl of Glencairn's attempted uprising in 1651. In recognition of this loyalty, Charles II repealed the measures after the Restoration, but they were swiftly reimposed by William III, after he ascended the throne in 1688.

ROB ROY'S GRAVE *The hero of Scott's novel had a farm at Balquhidder and is buried in the local churchyard.*

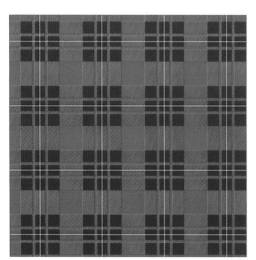

MACGREGOR *There is a sample of this tartan in the Cockburn Collection, Glasgow, dated 1815.*

This was the predicament which faced the most famous member of the clan, Rob Roy MacGregor (1671-1734). He was the son of Donald MacGregor of Glengyle, a lieutenant-colonel in James VII's forces but, after the renewal of the proscription, he adopted his mother's maiden name, Campbell. In Sir Walter Scott's novel (1817), Rob Roy was portrayed as a kind of Robin Hood figure, though the truth was rather less romantic. He was actually a cattle drover, buying and selling cattle on behalf of the Duke of Montrose. Then, following a claim that he had absconded with some money, Rob was outlawed and became a cattle thief (1712). He made a particular point of stealing from his former employer. He also ran a form of protection racket,

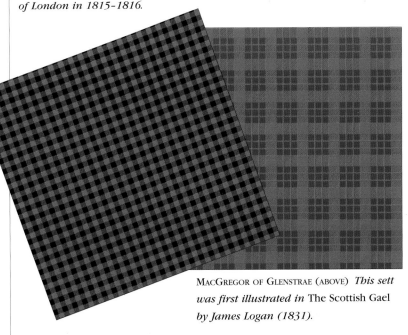

ROB ROY (BELOW) *A specimen of this simple tartan was lodged with the Highland Society of London in 1815-1816.*

MACGREGOR OF GLENSTRAE (ABOVE) *This sett was first illustrated in* The Scottish Gael *by James Logan (1831).*

LOCH KATRINE *Rob Roy MacGregor was born at Glen Gyle House, situated at the head of Loch Katrine.*

charging farmers a percentage of their rent to ensure that he left their herds alone. In these practices, Rob Roy enjoyed the protection of Montrose's enemy, the Duke of Argyll.

Rob Roy joined the Jacobite rebellion in 1715, although some considered that his support was half-hearted. At the Battle of Sheriffmuir, for example, it was said that he kept some distance from the fighting, waiting to see which side would gain the day and offer the best chance of booty. After the rising, Rob resumed his private quarrel with the Duke of Montrose and eventually died peacefully at home. According to one source, he learned on his deathbed that a former adversary was coming to visit him. Swiftly, he raised himself up and called for his claymore and pistols. 'For,' he declared, 'it must never be said that an enemy saw Rob Roy MacGregor defenceless and unarmed'.

MacInroy

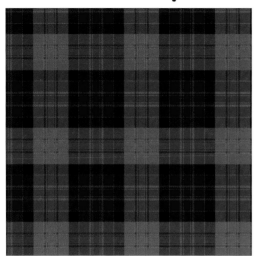

First published in Smith's Authenticated Tartans of the Clans of Scotland *(1850).*

THE MACINROYS are a recognized sept of the Clann Donnchaidh or Robertsons. Their name comes from the Gaelic *Mac Ian Ruaidh* ('Son of John Roy'). The earliest reference to the family dates from 1556, when a Makeanroy was cited in a document. The name was sometimes confused with MacInreoch (from *An Riabhach*, meaning 'the brindled one'), which featured in a number of 16th- and 17th-century documents. In 1613, for example, John Dow McInriache of Tomachlaganr and Muldonich McInriauch of Glenlyon were fined for harbouring members of the outlawed MacGregor clan. *An Rhiabhach* was also a common nickname for the devil.

MacIntyre

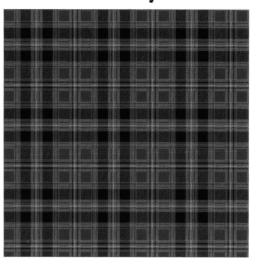

First recorded by W. & A. Smith, who described it as MacIntyre of Whitehouse (1850).

THE NAME IS thought to come from the Gaelic *Mac-an-T'saoir*, meaning 'Son of the Carpenter'. Their earliest homeland appears to have been at Glenoe, on Loch Etive. The MacIntyres were there from the 13th century, acting as hereditary foresters to the Stewarts of Lorn. Other branches of the clan were hereditary pipers to the MacDonalds of Clanranald and the Menzies, while the MacIntryes of Cladich were famed for their weaving skills. Perhaps the most celebrated individual was Duncan MacIntyre (1724–1812), the clan bard. He was jailed after Culloden, for verses which criticized the ban on Highland dress.

MacIver

This first appeared in The Scottish Clans and Their Tartans *(1891).*

APPARENTLY THE MACIVERS originated in the Glen Lyon district of Perthshire, but travelled westwards in Alexander II's army, when he went to quell a revolt in Argyllshire in 1221. The far west still owed its primary allegiance to Norway, so the king was keen to install his supporters in the area and, accordingly, he rewarded the MacIvers with lands in Lergachonzie and Asknish. Little is known of their fortunes in the following centuries and, for a time, they appear to have been a broken clan. In 1688, the MacIvers were forced to take the name of Campbell, as punishment for Iver of Asknish's part in a rebellion.

MacKay

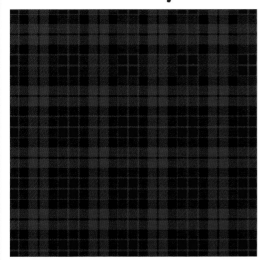

*The clan chief presented this pattern to the
Highland Society of London in 1816.*

THIS IS AN ancient clan, sometimes known as the Clan Morgan or the Clan Aoidh. Neither of these ancestors can be identified with any certainty, but the former may be a 14th-century figure - Morgan, son of Magnus - who also had a grandson called Aoidh (Hugh). The first recorded chief was Angus Dubh, who married the sister of the Lord of the Isles in *c*.1415 and was killed in the Battle of Drumnacoub (1429). Angus's power was considerable, for it was said that he could raise an army of 4,000 men from his lands at Strathnaver. His descendant, Sir Donald MacKay exerted similar power and was made Lord Reay in 1628.

MACKENZIE SEE PAGE **89**

MacKellar

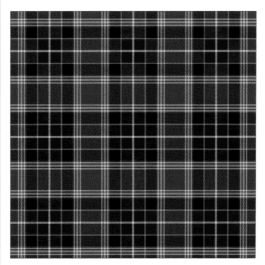

*A modern tartan, used by this sept
of the Campbells.*

MACKELLAR DERIVES from the Gaelic *Mac Ealair* ('Son of Hilary'). This, in turn, comes from the French saint (*c*.315–*c*.368), who gave his name to the Hilary term in British law courts and universities. There are several figures called Hilarius in medieval Scottish documents, but the earliest references to MacKellar date from the 15th century. In 1436, Patrick McKellar witnessed a charter at Carnasserie. Archibald Makelar of Argyll, 'a Scottyshman', was granted safe conduct to England (1488), and Gilmertine MacEllere was involved in the murder of the laird of Calder (1594). Archibald McKellar (1844-1901) was a noted US sculptor, while Kenneth McKellar is a popular Scottish tenor.

Mackinlay

*Similar to the Black Watch tartan, this
dates back to 1906.*

ORIGINALLY, THE MacKinlays came from the Lennox district, around Loch Lomond, but their early history is poorly documented. The first account was provided by Buchanan of Auchmar in 1723. He affirmed that the Lennox Mackinlays were descended from Finlay, a son of Buchanan of Drumikill. As a result, Finlay and Finlayson became variants of the clan name. Many Mackinlays moved to Ulster in the early 17th century, joining the newly-created settlements. These 'plantations' were encouraged by the English government, as a means of introducing loyal, Protestant stock into the country. The most famous offspring from this branch was William McKinley, 25th President of the USA.

Mackenzie

THE NAME MEANS 'Son of Kenneth' or, in its Gaelic form, *MacCoinneach* ('Son of the Fair One'). Legend has it that the clan has Celtic roots, descending from the House of Lorn, but the early history of the family is very unclear. By 1270, however, they appear to have established themselves in the area around Eilean Donan, a vital stronghold at the mouth of Loch Duich. King Haakon's campaigns in the west were still fresh in the mind and, even though the Norwegian king had been defeated at the Battle of Largs (1263), the threat of renewed violence still loomed large. For this reason, perhaps, the Mackenzies

LEOD CASTLE (LEFT) *Although named after a MacLeod, the castle has always been a Mackenzie stronghold.*

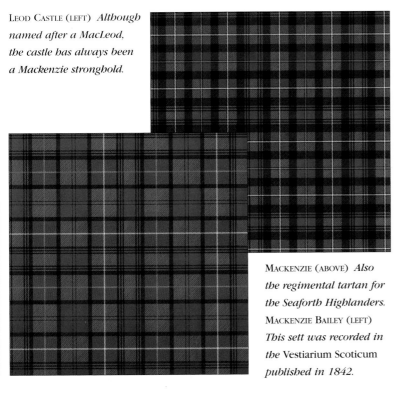

MACKENZIE (ABOVE) *Also the regimental tartan for the Seaforth Highlanders.*
MACKENZIE BAILEY (LEFT) *This sett was recorded in the* Vestiarium Scoticum *published in 1842.*

were made part of the royal bodyguard and Colin Mackenzie was granted land in Kintail.

The first secure reference to the family dates from 1427, when Alexander Ionraech, 7th Chief of Kintail, was summoned to Parliament by James I. In 1491, the clan won a victory over the MacDonalds at Blair-na-Park and, in 1513, John of Kintail supported James IV at Flodden. Colin, 11th Chief, is said to have fought for Mary Queen of Scots at Langside (1568), although he acknowledged James VI in the following year.

The Mackenzies were made Lords of Kintail in 1609, Earls of Seaforth in 1623, and Earls of Cromartie in 1702. In the west, they still controlled Eilean Donan. They also owned Leod Castle, completed by Sir Rory Mackenzie after his marriage to Margaret MacLeod. Through her, Rory acquired MacLeod estates in Lewis (1616). He also became one of the Nova Scotia Baronets in 1628.

The Mackenzies have made their mark in many fields. Sir Alexander Mackenzie (1764-1820) was a noted explorer in north-west Canada. The Mackenzie River is named after him. Alexander Mackenzie (1822-1892) was a Canadian statesman, the first Liberal Prime Minister of the Dominion (1873-1878). Sir Compton Mackenzie (1883-1972) was a successful novelist, best remembered for *Whisky Galore* (1947).

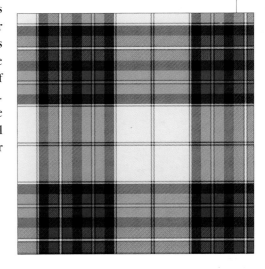

MACKENZIE DRESS *A sample of this tartan was included in Paton's collection, assembled in the 1830s.*

Mackinnon

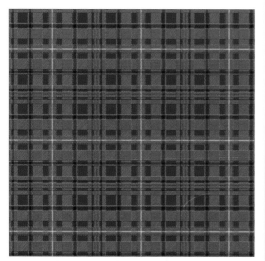

*This version of the tartan was certified by
the Highland Society of London in 1816.*

THE MACKINNONS began as a branch of the MacAlpine clan. Their name means 'Son of Fingon', indicating that they were descended from one of the younger sons of King Alpin. From a very early stage, they were based in Skye and Mull. On the former, Findanus, 4th Chief, acquired Dun Akin ('Haakon's fort'; now Castle Moil) by marrying a Norse princess, and levied tolls on passing ships. Several members of the family became abbots of Iona, the last of these being John Mackinnon, 9th Chief, who was also Bishop of the Isles (*c.*1500). The Mackinnons supported the Stuarts during the Civil War and were 'out' in the two Jacobite uprisings, fighting at both Sheriffmuir and Culloden.

Mackintosh

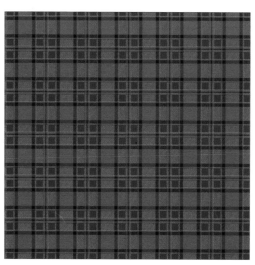

*First documented by Logan in 1831, though
it is known to be much older.*

THE MACKINTOSH clan (literally 'Son of the Chief') is thought to descend from Shaw MacDuff, a younger son of the Earl of Fife. He was made Constable of Inverness Castle in *c.*1163, gaining the nearby lands of Petty. In 1291, the family fortunes were boosted by a marriage between Angus, 6th Chief, and Eva, the heiress of Clan Chattan, and the Mackintoshes became leaders of this confederation. In later years, there were damaging feuds with the Gordons and the Camerons, but the clan gained renown for the Rout of Moy (1746), when Lady Mackintosh, nicknamed 'Colonel' Anne, tricked a force of 1,500 Government troops into fleeing from a handful of her retainers.

MacKirdy

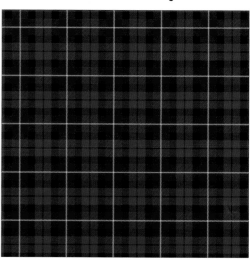

*A modern tartan, included in the
MacGregor-Hastie Collection (c.1930-1950).*

IN ITS MANY different forms, this surname is common on the islands of Bute and Arran. The family are regarded as a sept of the Stuarts of Bute and, for a time, they leased much of the island from James IV (ruled 1488-1513). In 1506, Gilcrist Makwrerdy owned the lands of Bransar on Bute, while Sir James M'Wartye, a papal knight, was vicar of Kingarth (1554-1556). At the end of the century, James Makilveritie held the post of chaplain at Rothesay Castle. In addition, the name of Myrkjartan is cited in several of the Icelandic sagas. Alternative spellings include MacCurdy, McQuhirertie, M'Urartys, and MacVurarthie.

MacLachlan

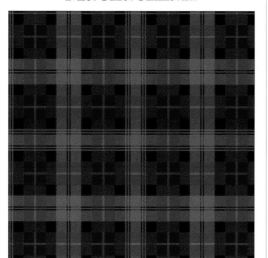

Recorded by T. Smibert in The Clans of
the Highlands of Scotland *(1850).*

MACLACHLAN APPEARS in Scotland from the 13th century, when Lachlan Mor was cited as a great warrior chieftain. Ewen MacLachlan was a signatory of the Ragman Rolls (1296), while Gillespie MacLachlan was a member of Bruce's first Parliament (1308). The clan lands were centred on Strathlachlan, though the family owned considerable estates throughout Argyllshire. The MacLachlans were active in both Jacobite risings, and the chief was appointed Bonnie Prince Charlie's aide-de-camp. He died at Culloden and his former possessions were briefly confiscated, before being restored to his son, Robert, in 1749.

MacLaine of Lochbuie

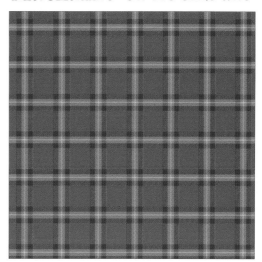

*This pattern, preserved in the Cockburn
Collection, dates back to at least 1810.*

THE CLAN NAME derives from MacGhille-Eain or 'Son of Gillean'. This refers to a fearsome, 13th-century warrior, Gillean of the Battleaxe, who was also the ancestor of the MacLeans. The two lines separated in the following century, after Eachainn Reaganach (Hector the Stern) was granted the lands of Lochbuie, on Mull (1350). Both branches of the family were spelled 'MacLean' until the 16th century, though this did not prevent them from feuding. In 1773, John, 17th Chief, played host to Dr Johnson and Boswell at Lochbuie, during their travels in the Hebrides. The visitors found the chief an engaging eccentric, describing him as 'a bluff, comely, noisy old gentleman'.

MacLaren

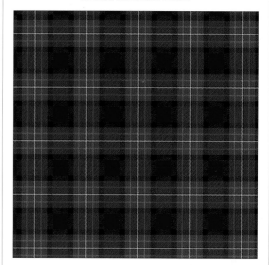

*Wilson was producing this tartan before 1820,
selling it under the name of 'Regent'.*

TWO UNCONNECTED branches of this clan exist. By tradition, the MacLarens of Argyll are descended from Lorn, one of the sons of Fergus Mór, who founded Dalriada in the early 6th century. Through him, they came to own the island of Tiree. The Perthshire MacLarens, cite Laurence, a 13th-century abbot of Achtow, in Balquhidder as their ancestor. Strathearn and Balquhidder were the family estates, although they had lost both by the end of the 14th century, becoming tenants rather than landowners. The clan were at Culloden, where Donald MacLaren was taken by the English. He made a dramatic escape, however, which Scott recounted in *Redgauntlet*.

MacLeod

B Y ALL ACCOUNTS, the MacLeods are descended from Leod, son of Olaf the Black (died *c.*1237), who was one of the last Norse kings of the Isle of Man and the Northern Isles. Leod inherited Harris and Lewis, and also acquired part of Skye through his marriage to the daughter of the island's Norse seneschal. He had four sons, two of whom founded the principal branches of the MacLeods. Tormod, the eldest, was the ancestor of the MacLeods of Skye. He was given the castle of Dunvegan, which is still the main seat of the clan, and the island of Harris. Leod's second son, Torquil, headed the MacLeods of Lewis (traditionally called 'MacLeods of the Lewes'). The MacLeods of Raasay were a later offshoot from this line.

Leod and his children lived at a pivotal period in the history of the Isles. King Haakon's abortive invasion attempt ended in disaster at the Battle of Largs (1263) and Norwegian influence in the west began to wane. By the Treaty of Perth (1266), Norway ceded the Western Isles to Scotland for a payment of 4,000 marks. After this, the Lords of the Isles – the MacDonalds – became the dominant force in the area. The early MacLeods served under them, though they had to steer a careful path between the conflicting ambitions of the MacDonalds and the Scottish Crown.

NORMAN MACLEOD *A portrait of the 22nd Chief by Allan Ramsay. He is wearing tartan trews, rather than a kilt.*

Tormod's people supported Robert the Bruce in the wars against the English and his son, Malcolm, was granted the lands of Glenelg by David II (*c.*1343). The king also gave the MacLeods of Lewis a charter for the Barony of Assynt, in Sutherland. In 1411, the clan supported the Lord of the Isles at the Battle of Harlaw, but relations with the MacDonalds were later soured by a feud. As a result of this, William, 7th Chief, perished at the Battle of the Bloody Bay.

His successor, Alasdair Crotach ('Hump-backed'), revived the fortunes of the MacLeods. He captured Duntulm Castle, on the island of Skye, and acquired legal rights to the lands of Trotternish, which had also been claimed by the MacDonalds of Sleat. He is most celebrated, however, for his impertinent wager with James V. During the course of a royal visit, Alasdair bet the king that he could show his guest a finer

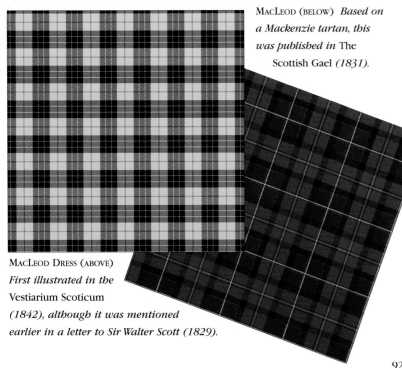

MACLEOD (BELOW) *Based on a Mackenzie tartan, this was published in* The Scottish Gael *(1831).*

MACLEOD DRESS (ABOVE) *First illustrated in the* Vestiarium Scoticum *(1842), although it was mentioned earlier in a letter to Sir Walter Scott (1829).*

92

table and candlesticks, than any at his Court. James took up the challenge and Alasdair prepared a sumptuous banquet, on a scenic, flat-topped hill above Dunvegan Castle. The 'candlesticks' were provided by his clansmen, dressed in their finest apparel, who held up a row of flaming torches. The king graciously admitted defeat.

The next great leader of the clan was Rory Mor, 16th Chief, who was knighted by James VI in 1603. He enlarged Dunvegan Castle, recovered some clan lands that had been forfeited, built roads and schools, imported grain when the harvest was bad, and settled the long-running dispute with the MacDonalds by marrying a daughter of the Chief of Glengarry. After his death, a famous pibroch ('Rory Mor's Lament') was composed in his honour by Patrick Mor MacCrimmon. In addition, an enormous drinking horn named after him is still occasionally used as an initiation test for aspiring chiefs. In theory, the candidate is supposed to drain the horn – which can hold a bottle and a half of claret – in a single draught.

Most MacLeods supported the Royalist cause during the Civil War, and five hundred clansmen were lost in the disastrous defeat at Worcester (1651). Nevertheless, the most abiding association of this era is with a terrible act of betrayal. In 1650, after his army had been scattered at Carbisdale, the Marquis of Montrose fled to the Highlands. There, exhausted and half-starved, he came across Neil MacLeod, the Laird of Assynt, who had

RAASAY *The MacLeods sheltered Bonnie Prince Charlie for two nights on Raasay and, in punishment, Government troops laid waste to their estate on the island.*

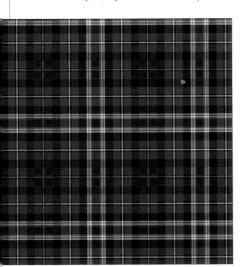

MACLEOD'S HIGHLANDERS *This regiment was raised in 1777 by Lord MacLeod, and the tartan was provided by Wilson's of Bannockburn.*

been one of his followers. Assynt fed him and gave him shelter at Ardvreck Castle, but then delivered him up to certain death by handing him over to Government forces. It was rumoured throughout Scotland that the laird accepted a reward of £25,000 for his treachery, but this has always been vehemently denied by the MacLeods.

A more auspicious reception awaited Dr Johnson and James Boswell, when they accepted the hospitality of the MacLeods. In 1773, they were entertained at Raasay House, during their Hebridean tour. They described the chief as 'the perfect representation of a Highland gentleman' and it proved to be one of their happiest stays. Boswell climbed the nearby hill of Dun Cann and danced a reel on its summit, while Johnson delighted in the company of MacLeod of Raasay's ten daughters, declaring them the best bred children that he ever saw.

MacLay

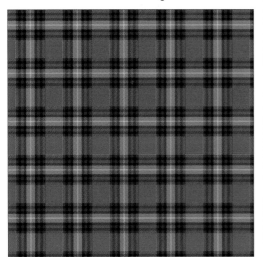

This tartan is also used by the Livingstones and resembles the sett of the Stewarts of Appin.

A FAMILY ASSOCIATED with the Stewarts of Appin, MacLay is an abbreviated form of *Mac Dhunnshleibhne* ('Son of Dunsleve', a popular forename meaning 'brown of the hill'). In 1518, the Clan MacDowleanis gave its bond to Sir John Campbell of Caldor, while Duncan M'Dunlewe was a minister in Kilmarnock (1541). The name became more recognizable in the 17th century. In the north, the family were known as the Clan Leajwe or the Makleys, while, further south, Donald M'Clae became a burgess of Glasgow in 1617, while Duncan McDonnslae was charged with assault and cattle-stealing (1623).

MacLean of Duart

This design is taken from The Scottish Gael, *compiled by James Logan (1831).*

LIKE THE MACLAINES, this clan traces its line back to Gillean of the Battleaxe. The MacLeans of Duart were recognized through tanistry as the senior branch of the clan. Marriage to the daughter of the Lord of the Isles brought the MacLeans extensive lands and influence in the West. Increasingly, though, they came under threat from the growing power of the Campbells. Their enmity was stirred by the attempt of one MacLean chief to drown his Campbell wife by marooning her on a tidal island. She was rescued by fishermen, however, and the husband was stabbed to death by his in-laws (1523).

MACLEOD SEE PAGES 92–93

MacLintock

A sett from the MacGregor-Hastie Collection (c. 1930–1950).

THE MACLINTOCKS are a sept of the MacDougalls. They take their name from *Mac Ghill Fhionndaig* ('Son of the Servant of Fintan'). There were several Irish saints with the name of Fintan, but the one with the closest Scottish connections was Fintan Munnu (d.635), who travelled to Iona shortly after Columba's death. The surname was common in the area around Luss and the district of Lorn. A poet named M'Gillindak wrote some of the verses in the Dean of Lismore's Book, and Duncan McGellentak was cited as a witness in a document from Balquhidder (1549). At the end of the 17th century, James Mcillandaig became the last of the Breadalbane smugglers.

Macmillan

This pattern comes from The Tartans of the Clans and Septs of Scotland, *published in 1906.*

THE ORIGIN OF the clan is ecclesiastical. The name *MacMhaoil-Iain* means 'Son of the Tonsured One'. More precisely, the suffix Iain indicates the Celtic tonsure of St John, rather than the Roman version. The Macmillans were present in several areas, most notably the Loch Arkaig district in Lochaber, where they had settled by the 12th century. Other branches were located in Argyll and Galloway. The leading family members were Kirkpatrick Macmillan (1813-1878), the inventor of the bicycle, and Sir Harold Macmillan (1894-1986), the British Prime Minister.

MacNab

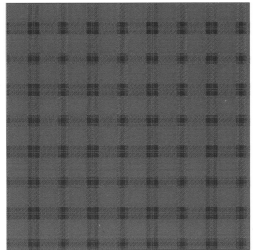

The pattern is identical to the Black Watch tartan, but in different colours.

MACNAB MEANS 'Son of the Abbot', a reference to the clan's descent from the abbots of Glendochart, in Perthshire. Tradition links the family with Abraruadh, the Red Abbot, one of King Kenneth MacAlpin's sons (ruled 843-859). The MacNabs lost many of their lands after opposing Robert the Bruce, following his murder of their relative, Red Comyn, but some of these were restored under David II (1336). Later, 'Smooth John' MacNab gained fame for his exploits with Montrose (1640s) and his daring escape from capture; while Archibald MacNab fled to Canada to escape his debts (1823), founding the settlement of MacNab, by the Ottawa River.

MacNaughton

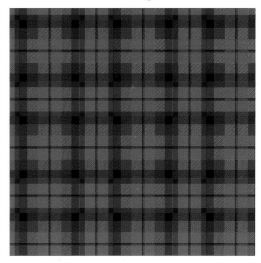

Recorded by Logan in 1831, this tartan is also worn by the Vale of Atholl pipe band.

BY TRADITION, THE MacNaughtons ('Sons of Nechtan') claim descent from the ancient Picts, for several of their rulers went by this name. Twelfth-century records linked them with Strathtay, describing them as Thanes of Loch Tay. Then, in 1267, Alexander III appointed Gilchrist MacNachten as keeper of the Castle of Fraoch Eilean, by Loch Awe. The clan fortunes suffered, when they took up arms against Bruce, but in the 14th century they acquired their chief stronghold, Dunderave, on Loch Fyne. The MacNaughtons were fervent supporters of the Stuarts. Alexander was knighted by Charles II in 1660 and his successor fought for the Jacobites at Killiecrankie (1689).

MacNeil

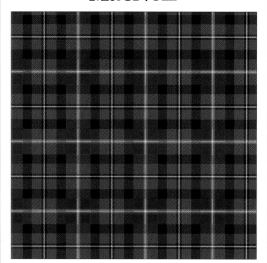

This sett is taken from Stewart's Old &
Rare Scottish Tartans *(1893).*

THE MACNEILS are of Irish lineage, claiming as their ancestor Aodh O'Neil, ruler of the north of Ireland (1030-1033) and a descendant of the powerful Uí Néill dynasty. In *c.*1049, he settled in Barra, which became the heartland of the MacNeil clan. The 5th Chief was a member of the Council of the Isles in 1252 and Gilleonan, 9th Chief, received a charter for Barra and Boisdale, South Uist, in 1427. Their most troublesome descendant was Ruari, 15th Chief, nicknamed 'Rory the Tartar'. From his stronghold at Kisimul, he led a life of piracy until his nephews imprisoned him (1610). The MacNeils of Gigha and Colonsay were also prominent branches of the clan.

MacNicol

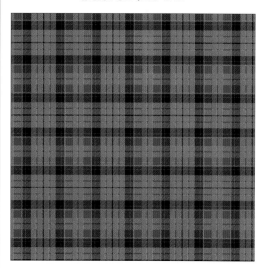

Published in the Authenticated Tartans of the Clans
and Families of Scotland *(1850).*

THE HISTORY OF the MacNicols and the Nicolsons is closely intertwined. They have the same tartan and very similar heraldry. The name itself is probably of Norse origin. It may be a combination of 'Nic' (Gaelic for 'daughter of') and the forename 'Olsen', or it may be a corruption of Nicolassen. Significantly, the MacNicol lands - initially at Assynt, near Ullapool, and later on Skye - were in territory that had been settled by Viking raiders.

LOCH BROOM *The first MacNicol lands were on the northern shores of Loch Broom, which the chief, Mackrycul, held as a vassal of the Thanes of Sutherland.*

MacPhail

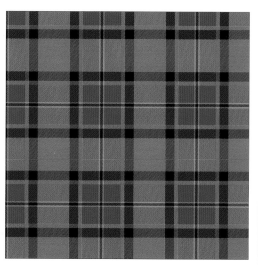

*One of the samples in the MacGregor-Hastie
Collection (c.1930-1950).*

MEANING 'Son of Paul', the name can be found in a variety of forms. These include MacVail, MacFaul, MacPhiel and, in its most anglicized state, Polson. The family are said to be a branch of the Mackays, tracing their line back to Paul, son of Neil MacNeil Mackay, in the early 15th century. They are also associated with the Camerons. In 1414, Gillemore M'Phale attended an inquest at Inverness, while Niven M'Phaill witnessed a charter at Sonnachan (1488). The name was common in the area around Ardchattan and Glenlyon, where several men enrolled in the Fencible company raised by the Duke of Atholl (1706).

Macpherson

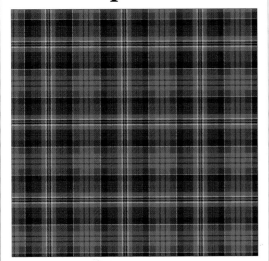

This is a design used by the weavers, Bolingbroke & Jones of Norwich, in c.1870.

THE MACPHERSONS CLAIM to trace their line back to Gille Chattan Mor, a 9th-century Chief of the Clan Chattan Confederation. Their name, which means 'Son of the Parson', comes from one of his descendants, Muireach Cattenach, who was parson of Kingussie in 1173. In the aftermath of the '45 Rebellion, Ewen Macpherson eluded Government troops for nine years, despite having a reward of £1,000 on his head.

STRATHSPEY *James Macpherson (1736-1796), who lived nearby, concocted a highly-successful book of romantic Celtic tales, supposedly written by an ancient poet named Ossian.*

MacQuarrie

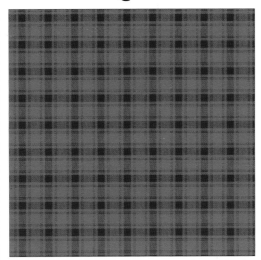

This pattern was recorded by Grant (1886), although an earlier variant is known (1815).

IT IS POSSIBLE that the MacQuarrie name comes from Godfrey (Guarie), a great-grandson of Kenneth MacAlpin. The earliest documentary evidence, however, dates from 1473, when the death of John Macquarrie was recorded. At this stage, the clan lands included the island of Ulva and part of Mull. At different times, the MacQuarries followed the MacDonalds or the MacLeans of Duart, but they were badly affected by the defeat at Inverkeithing (1651), when the clan was almost wiped out. Lachlan Macquarie (1761-1824) became Governor of New South Wales in 1809, transforming it from a penal settlement into a thriving colony.

MacQueen

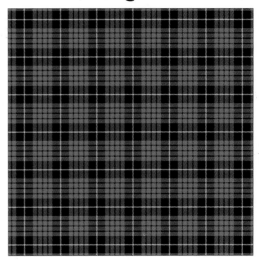

First recorded in the Vestiarium Scoticum, *which was published in 1842.*

MACQUEEN AND MacSween both derive from Sweyn, a common Norse name. The earliest record of the family dates from the 13th century, when the MacSweens were confirmed as custodians of Castle Sween, in Argyllshire. They also held property in Skye and Lewis, later acquiring the lands of Corrybrough, their principal estate. The MacQueens maintained close links with the Mackintoshes and, through them, became a sept of the Clan Chattan. Accordingly, their chiefs were signatories of the Clan Chattan Bonds of Union in 1609 and 1664. The MacQueens lost Corrybrough in the 18th century, but the Lanarkshire branch of the family grew in prominence.

MacRae

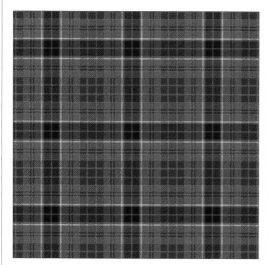

From Authenticated Tartans of the Clans
and Families of Scotland *(1850)*.

MACRAE MEANS 'Son of Grace', which suggests that the clan's origins were ecclesiastical. Early records place them in Clunes, near Beauly. By the 14th century, however, they were established in their traditional heartland - Kintail, at the head of Loch Duich. There, they proved loyal supporters of the Mackenzies, earning the nickname of 'the Mackenzies' shirt of mail'. As part of their duties, they were Constables of Eilean Donan Castle. Notable family members have included Donnachadh nam Pios ('Duncan of the Silver Cups'), who compiled the Fernaig Manuscript (1688-1693), an important anthology of Gaelic verse, and James MacRae (1677-1744), Governor of Madras.

MacTaggart

*One of the tartans from Paton's Collection,
assembled in the 1830s.*

DEPENDANTS OF the Ross clan, the name MacTaggart comes from the Gaelic *Mac an t'sagairt* ('Son of the Priest'). A notable figure was Ferchar Mackinsagart, the son of the red priest of Applecross, who was rewarded with a knighthood by Alexander II (1215), after suppressing a rebellion in Morayshire. In more recent times, the MacTaggarts were a distinguished family of Scottish artists. William McTaggart (1835-1910) was one of the leading landscape painters of his day, as was his grandson, Sir William MacTaggart (1903-1981). The latter became President of the Royal Scottish Academy (1959-1964) and was made a Chevalier of the Légion d'honneur in 1968.

MacTavish

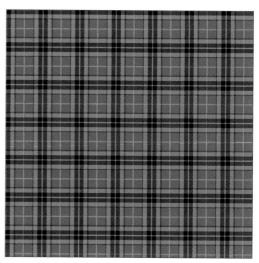

First recorded in The Tartans of the Clans
and Septs of Scotland *(1906)*.

THIS FAMILY IS mainly associated with the Campbells, although the MacTavishes of Stratherrick are considered a sept of the Frasers. Their name comes from the Gaelic *Mac Tamhais*, which means 'Son of Tammas' (the Lowland form of 'Thomas'). As a result, there are close connections with the Thomsons. The MacTavishes are said to be descended from Tavis Corr, an illegitimate son of Gillespick. Their ancestral seat is on the lands of Dunardry, which was gained by charter in the 14th century. The clan supported the Jacobite cause, fighting in the ranks of the Mackintoshes, as their own chief had been imprisoned in 1745 on the orders of the Duke of Argyll.

MacThomas

*A modern tartan, this pattern was adopted
by the MacThomas Clan Society in 1975.*

INITIALLY, THIS CLAN was a branch of the Clan Chattan Mackintoshes. Then, in the 15th century, Tomaidh Mor and his kinsmen formed a new settlement at Glen Shee, in Perthshire. The descendants of Tomaidh became known as MacThomas or McComie, the phonetic equivalent in Gaelic. The clan played a prominent role in the Civil War. Initially, John McComie, 7th Chief, supported the Royalists, fighting alongside Montrose in 1644. Later, however, he switched allegiance and the family suffered badly after the Restoration. By the end of the century the clan was drifting apart, with some members moving to Angus or Fife. Here, they were known as Thom, Thomas, or Thomson.

MacWhirter

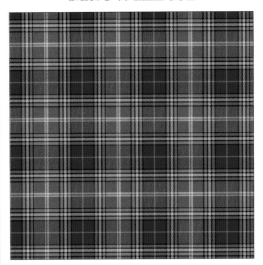

*The earliest known source is W. & A.
Smith's book of tartans (1850).*

THE FAMILY IS traditionally linked with the Buchanans. The name itself is an alternate form of MacChruiter, which means 'Son of the Harper'. In the Highlands, this was an important, hereditary post and records date back to the 14th century. In 1346, David II granted land to Patrick M'Churteer, son of the harper of Carrick. The Reverend Alexander McWhorter (1734-1807) played a part in the American Revolution, later becoming a trustee of the College of New Jersey (now Princeton). In 1955, the hugely successful *Guiness Book of Records* was created by twin brothers, Ross (1925-1975) and Norris (b.1925) McWhirter.

MacWilliam

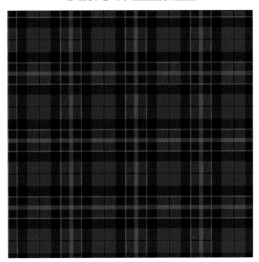

First illustrated in the Clan Originaux,
published in Paris in 1880.

CLOSELY ASSOCIATED with the Gunns and the MacFarlanes, MacWilliam ('Son of William') can be found in many parts of Scotland. One particular branch, however, came close to gaining the Scottish throne. These were the great-grandsons of Malcolm III, who reigned from 1058 to 1093. By his first wife, Ingeborg of Orkney, Malcolm had a son named Duncan, who ruled briefly (1094), before being murdered. The succession then passed to the children of his second marriage. Duncan's son, William, was too young to challenge for the throne, but his children, the MacWilliams, made a series of unsuccessful attempts to seize the crown back from William the Lion (1165-1214).

Maitland

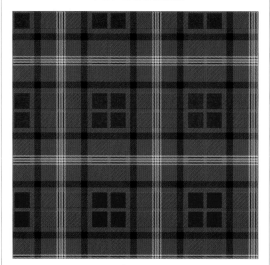

Approved in 1960, this tartan can only
be worn by the chief of the clan.

AN ANGLO-NORMAN family, the Maitlands settled in Northumberland after the Conquest, before moving to Scotland. In the mid-13th century, Sir Richard Matulant held considerable estates in the Borders, most notably at Thirlestane. Under the Stuarts, William Maitland gained fame as Mary Queen of Scots' secretary and confidant, while his successor was made Earl of Lauderdale in 1616. John, 2nd Earl, rose even higher, becoming Secretary of State and Lord High Commissioner to Parliament. He also gained a dukedom (1672) and transformed Thirlestane into a veritable palace. The family are the hereditary bearers of the Scottish flag on State occasions.

Makgill

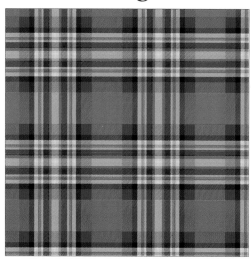

This tartan belongs to a Lowland clan, most
prominent in Galloway and Fife.

THE NAME IS thought to derive from the Gaelic *Mac an ghoill* ('Son of the Lowlander'). Initially, the family seems to have been based in Galloway and, in 1231, Maurice Macgeil was witness to a charter. In the 16th century, however, they became established in the east, when Sir James Makgill purchased the lands of Nether Rankeillour, in Fife. He was an influential figure – Provost of Edinburgh, a supporter of John Knox, and a Privy Councillor under Mary Queen of Scots – though he eventually fell from favour, following his involvement in the murder of Rizzio. A later Sir James gained the titles of Baronet of Nova Scotia (1627) and Viscount Oxfuird (1651).

Malcolm

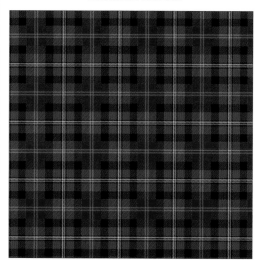

First recorded in Smith's Authenticated Tartans
of the Clans and Families of Scotland *(1850).*

LIKE MACCALLUM, the name designates a disciple of St Columba. Indeed, Malcolm is simply the anglicized form of Calum and, as a result, the two names were virtually interchangeable in many early documents. Nevertheless, before 1200, there were four Scottish kings with this name, including the one who deposed Macbeth in 1057 (Malcolm III). Much later, in 1641, John Malcolm of Baldedie, Lochore, and Innerneil became Chamberlain of Fife. It was only after Dugald MacCallum changed his name to Malcolm (c.1779), however, that the distinction between the two clans grew more evident.

Mar

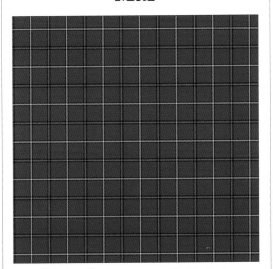

This is a district tartan, probably dating from around 1850.

THE LANDS OF Mar are in Aberdeenshire, between the Rivers Don and Dee. In early Scottish history, this was one of the seven petty kingdoms governed by a mormaer (literally 'great steward', but roughly equivalent to a thane or earl). Rothri, 1st Earl of Mar, was mentioned in a charter of 1114, William, 5th Earl, was both Regent and Lord Chamberlain of Scotland (1264), while Isabella of Mar married Robert the Bruce and was the grandmother of Robert II. The earldom became the subject of a long-running dispute, after the Erskines claimed the title. In 1875, the House of Lords ruled that the Earl of Mar and Kellie (the Erskine Chief) was distinct from the Chief of the Tribe of Mar.

Matheson

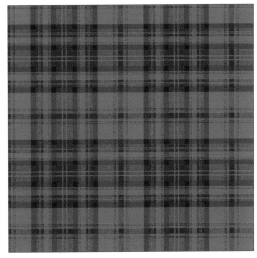

This sett is from Smith (1850), although earlier versions have also been recorded.

MATHESON PROBABLY comes from the Gaelic MacMathan ('Son of the Bear'). The clan is first recorded in the west, where it was granted the lands of Lochalsh and Kintail by the Earl of Ross. Kenneth MacMathan, constable of Eilean Donan Castle, joined Alexander III's expedition against the Norsemen of the Isles (1262). Their star rose quickly and, by the early 15th century, the Chief of the Mathesons was said to have 2,000 men at his command. The other main branch of the family lived at Shiness, Sutherland. Their leading member was James Sutherland Matheson, benefactor of Lewis and co-founder of Jardine, Matheson & Co.

Maxwell

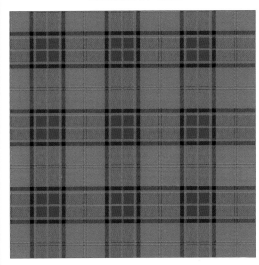

The tartan of this Border clan was first recorded in the Vestiarium Scoticum.

THERE IS A tradition that the clan takes its name from Maccus, an 11th-century ruler of Man and the Western Isles, but this is probably without foundation. Instead, the family appear to have begun as Norman settlers in the Borders. Sir John Maxwell (d.1241), who was Chamberlain of Scotland, is the first recorded ancestor. His descendant, Herbert, was created Lord Maxwell in *c.*1445 and the title of Earl of Nithsdale was added in *c.*1613. One of the earliest strongholds of the clan was Caerlaverock Castle, which Sir Eustace Maxwell took from the English in 1312, and the family also owned Pollok House, near Glasgow, which is now the home of the Burrell Collection.

Menzies

Originally mistaken for a MacFarlane tartan, this sample is from the Cockburn Collection (c.1815).

FROM NORMAN STOCK, the Menzies clan takes its name from Mesnières, near Rouen. The family gained prominence in both Scotland and England, where they were known as Manners. The Scottish line is descended from Sir Robert de Meyneris, who became Lord High Chamberlain in 1249. The clan supported Bruce at Bannockburn and was rewarded with the estates of Glendochart, Durisdeer, and Glenorchy.

LOCH RANNOCH *This Perthshire loch was in the heart of traditional Menzies' territory. Their chief stronghold, Castle Menzies, lay a few miles to the south, at Weem.*

Middleton

Illustrated in Johnston's Tartans of the Clans and Septs of Scotland *(1906).*

THE CLAN NAME has territorial origins, probably deriving from the lands of Middleton near Laurencekirk, in Kincardineshire. In 1296, Humfrey de Middleton signed the Ragman Rolls, while his kinsman, Robert, was involved in the siege of Dunbar Castle. The most distinguished family member, however, was John Middleton, the Civil War commander. He fought for the Royalists at the Battles of Preston (1648) and Worcester (1651), before escaping to the continent. He returned at the Restoration, when Charles II made him an earl. The title was later forfeited by his son, following an abortive attempt to depose William III.

Moffat

*Based on a Douglas pattern, this modern
tartan was recognized in 1983.*

MOFFAT WAS AN ancient Border clan, which probably gave its name to the town of Moffat in Dumfriesshire. Its origins are said to be Norse, but the earliest figure of note was Nicholas de Moffet, who was Bishop of Glasgow in 1268. At Bannockburn, Adam Moffat of Knock and his clansmen fought alongside Bruce and were rewarded with grants of land. Several of Adam's successors reached high office, most notably Walter de Moffet, Archdeacon of Lothian, who was made Ambassador to France in 1337. The Moffats also had a less palatable reputation, as ferocious Border reivers. Their most dangerous rivals were the Johnstones, who almost destroyed the clan in 1557.

Moncreiffe

*This simple design was first featured in
Wilson's pattern book (1819).*

THE CLAN TAKES its name from the Perthshire Barony of Moncreiffe (in Gaelic, *Monadh craoibhe* or 'Hill of the sacred bough'). It claims descent from Maldred (d.1045), the brother of King Duncan I, but the earliest documented links are with Sir Matthew de Muncrephe, whose estates were confirmed in a charter of 1248. Malcolm, 6th Laird, was a counsellor of James II, and his son was shield bearer and chamberlain to James III. The next laird was the founder of the three main branches of the family: the Moncreiffes of that ilk, the Moncreiffs of Tulliebole, and the Moncrieffs of Bandirran. Sir Iain Moncreiffe of that ilk (d.1985) was a distinguished herald and clan historian.

Montgomery

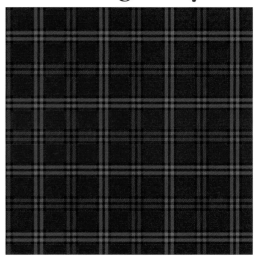

*First recorded by Stewart (1893), though it
is said to date back to 1707.*

THE MONTGOMERY CLAN was descended from a powerful Anglo-Norman family. A regent of Normandy, Roger de Mundegumbrie, joined the Conquest of England and was rewarded with an earldom. Almost a century later, Robert de Montgomerie arrived in Scotland, receiving the lands of Eaglesham in Renfrewshire. The family fortunes were greatly improved by Sir John, 7th Baron of Eaglesham, who distinguished himself at the Battle of Otterburn (1388) by capturing Harry Hotspur. He also married a wealthy heiress, thus gaining the lands of Eglinton and Ardrossan. In c.1449, Sir Alexander was created Lord Montgomery and the title of Earl of Eglinton was added to the family honours in 1507.

Morrison

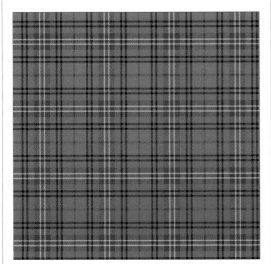

*Registered in 1968, this was based on a fragment
of tartan in an old family bible (1747).*

A PICTURESQUE legend tells how the first Morrison was a shipwrecked Norwegian prince, washed ashore on Lewis, clinging to a piece of driftwood. For all this, the Morrisons were not documented until the late 13th century, when they held the office of brieve (hereditary judge) on the island of Lewis. Although this important post gave them great prestige, the Morrisons suffered badly in clashes against the MacAulays and the Mackenzies, losing their Lewis estates in the late 16th century. A separate, Aberdeenshire branch of the clan came from Norman origins, taking its name from Maurice ('swarthy').

Mowat

First recorded in Clan Originaux, *published
in Paris in 1880.*

FOUNDED BY A Norman family, the clan settled initially in Wales and moved to Scotland during the reign of David I (1124-1153). Their name comes from *monthault* or, in its Latin form, *monte alto* ('high mountain'). It is found in a number of 13th-century charters. In *c.*1210, Robert de Muheut witnessed a document from the Earl of Buchan and, a few years later, William de Monte Alto signed a charter for Arbroath Abbey. The careers of several Mowats are linked with the sea. In 1281, Bernard de Monte Alto was drowned with Sir Patrick Spens, after accompanying Princess Margaret to Norway, while, in the 17th century, Axel Mowat became an admiral in the Norwegian navy.

Muir

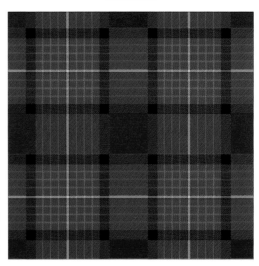

Documented in Land of the Scottish Gael
by John Ross (1930).

THERE ARE TWO possible derivations for the name Muir or More. In Gaelic, *mor* meant 'big' and was commonly used as an epithet. In Old English, the same word meant 'heath' or 'moor', and could be used to describe a family's estates. In Scotland, the chief branch of the clan were the Mures of Rowallan. Their lands were in Ayrshire, and their leading member was Gilchrist Mure who was knighted for his valour at the Battle of Largs (1263). His son, Archibald, was a casualty at the siege of Berwick, but a later descendant, Elizabeth Mure, married the future Robert II (1346).

MURRAY SEE PAGES 108–109

Murray

THE ACKNOWLEDGED ancestor of the clan was a 12th-century lord named Freskin, who received lands in Moray and West Lothian from David I. Moray was *Moireabh* in Gaelic and *Moravia* in Latin, and the name of Murray evolved from these. Freskin's own origins are uncertain. It is generally assumed that he was a Flemish adventurer, employed by the Normans to help subdue their new territories. Some claim, however, that he was of Pictish stock, a descendant of the ancient Mormaer of Moray.

Sir Walter de Moravia, one of Freskin's heirs, enlarged the family fortunes by marrying the heiress to the Bothwell estates in Clydesdale. A younger son of the Bothwell line became the founder of the Murrays of Tullibardine, ancestors of the Dukes of Atholl.

The most notable of the Murrays of Bothwell was Sir Andrew de Moray, who played a prominent role in the struggle against the English. He was Wallace's ablest lieutenant and, but for his untimely death at the Battle of Stirling Bridge (1297), independence might have been achieved far earlier. The Bothwell title passed to the Douglases in 1360, when the 5th Lord died of the plague.

After some friction, the chiefship passed to the Murrays of Tullibardine. Their line stretched back to 1282, when Sir William de Moravia acquired the estate through his marriage to the daughter of the Seneschal of Strathearn. The lands became a feudal barony in 1443 and Sir John, 12th Lord, was created Earl of Tullibardine in 1606. His son, William, enriched the clan still further by marrying Dorothea Stewart, daughter of the 5th Earl of Atholl. The latter had died without male issue and, as a result, the Murrays were able to claim the title. William's heirs were elevated to the rank of Marquess (1676) and then Duke of Atholl (1703). In 1736, the 2nd Duke inherited the sovereignty of the Isle of Man – a title which gave him the right to mint his own coins and preside over his own parliament.

BLAIR CASTLE *This noble house has long been the seat of the Murrays of Atholl. In 1745 it became the last castle in the British Isles to be laid under siege.*

MURRAY *This tartan was first illustrated in James Logan's* The Scottish Gael *(1831).*

MURRAY OF ATHOLL (RIGHT) *Also used as the Atholl district tartan.*

MURRAY OF TULLIBARDINE (ABOVE) *A pattern used by Wilson's, the regimental weavers (1819).*

Munro

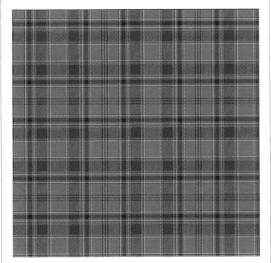

This sample is from the Cockburn Collection, housed in Glasgow (c.1810-1820).

THERE ARE CLAIMS that the ancestor of the clan was Hugh Munro (d.1126), but the first authenticated chief was Robert de Monro (d.1369). The clan gained a reputation for its fighting prowess, particularly under the leadership of Robert, the 'Black Baron'. He fought for Gustavus Adolphus in the Thirty Years' War (1618-1648), where his clansmen were dubbed 'the Invincibles'. Later notables include James Monroe, 5th President of the USA.

FOULIS CASTLE *A bizarre condition in the castle's charter stipulated that, if requested, the Munros had to pay the Crown a bucketful of snow on Midsummer's Day.*

Napier

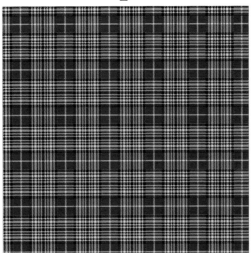

Published in The Setts of the Scottish Tartans *(1950), but similar to an older pattern.*

BY TRADITION, the Napiers are are said to be descended from an ancient Earl of Lennox's second son, Donald, who performed an act of heroism on the battlefield. His king congratulated him, saying that he had 'nae peer' ('no equal'). Before 1300 John de Naper was granted lands at Kilmahew in Dunbartonshire and later took part in the defence of Stirling Castle (1303). William was Governor of Edinburgh Castle (1401). Alexander, became Provost of the city in 1437 and acquired the lands of Merchiston, which became the family's Edinburgh seat. His most famous descendant was John, 8th Laird of Merchiston (1550-1617), the inventor of logarithms.

Nesbitt

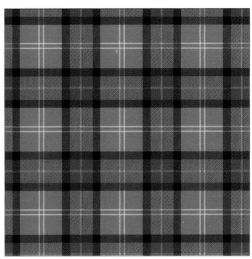

Registered in 1941, this is identical to an older Mackintosh sett (1842).

THIS BORDER clan takes its name from the Barony of Nesbit, in Berwickshire. In c.1160, William de Nesbite witnessed a charter relating to Coldingham Priory and his descendant, Thomas Nisbet, was a long-serving prior (1219-1240) at this religious house. The family lands were enlarged by Adam Nisbet of that ilk, who was granted the estate of Knocklies by Robert the Bruce. During the Civil War the clan fought valiantly for Charles I and Philip Nisbet was executed for the cause, following his capture at the Battle of Philiphaugh (1645). Another distinguished family member was Alexander Nisbet (1657-1725), whose *System of Heraldry* (1722) is still regarded as a seminal work.

Ogilvie

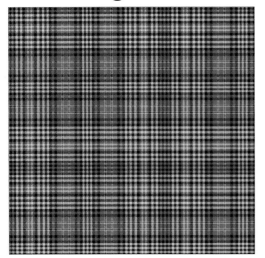

One of many Ogilvie tartans, this sample comes from the Highland Society of London.

THE OGILVIES were one of the seven mormaers (later earls), who ruled the ancient Pictish provinces. Their lands were in Angus and the name derives from *Ocel-fa* ('High Plain'). The acknowledged ancestor of the clan was Gilbert, Earl of Angus, who inherited the clan estates from his father, Gillebride, in *c.*1175. The Ogilvies acquired Cortachy and Airlie in the early 15th century. James, 7th Lord, was created Earl of Airlie in 1639, and the 2nd Earl narrowly escaped execution after the Battle of Philiphaugh (1645), by disguising himself in his sister's clothes. The family can also boast Scotland's only post-Reformation saint, St John Ogilvie (1579-1615), a martyred Jesuit priest.

Oliphant

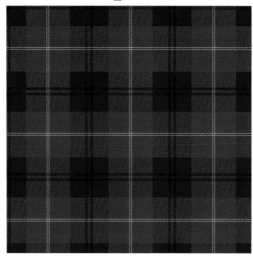

First published in the Vestiarium Scoticum *in 1842.*

AN ANGLO-NORMAN family originally based in Northampton. David de Olifard travelled to Scotland in the retinue of David I and was granted lands in Roxburghshire. Sir William Oliphant commanded Stirling Castle, during the siege by Edward I, and was a signatory of the Declaration of Arbroath (1320), Scotland's declaration of independence. These nationalist sentiments persisted through into the Jacobite era. The 9th Lord fought at Killiecrankie and the 10th Lord at Culloden. Carolina Oliphant (Baroness Nairne, 1766-1845) kept alive these memories in her spirited, Jacobite verses. She is best remembered for the lyrics of *Charlie is my Darling* and *Will ye no come back again*?

Rae

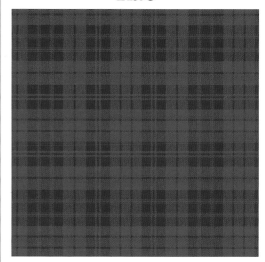

Wilson's made separate tartans for the Raes and the MacRaes, both dating from c.1819.

A BORDER FAMILY, the Raes flourished in Dumfriesshire in the 15th and 16th centuries. Prior to this, however, Robert Raa, a mason, witnessed a charter for the Abbey of Culross (*c.*1231). Another Robert, a burgess of Stirling, signed a land charter in *c.*1296, while William Raa, a former Bishop of Glasgow, died in 1367. A very distinguished member of the family was Dr John Rae (1813-1893), an intrepid Arctic explorer. He was born in the Orkneys and worked initially as a surgeon for the Hudson's Bay Company. In 1849, he joined the search for Sir John Franklin's expedition and, in the process, charted sections of north-west Canada, where there is a strait named after him.

Raeburn

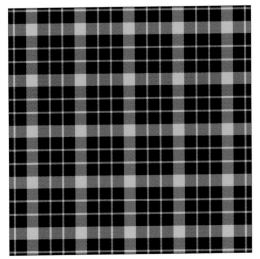

*A modern tartan, first noted in the trade
lists of Ross & Johnston (c.1930).*

THIS FAMILY TAKES its name from the lands of Ryburn, in the parish of Dunlop in Ayrshire. William of Raeburn witnessed a deed in 1331, while Andrew de Raburn became a burgess of Glasgow (1430). Thomas Reburne plied his trade as a goldsmith (1463) and, in the following century, his namesake gained the post of chaplain at Dornoch Cathedral (1544). Most famous of all was the portraitist, Sir Henry Raeburn (1756–1823), who painted Sir Walter Scott and many of his contemporaries. His career coincided with the revival of interest in tartan and many of his sitters chose to be depicted wearing Highland dress. The portrait of Alastair MacDonell is a fine example (see page 79).

Ramsay

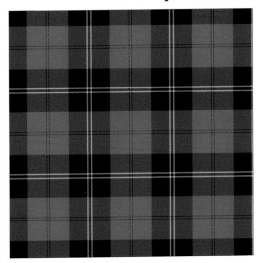

*Black replaces the crimson of earlier
versions in this 1906 tartan.*

AN ANGLO-NORMAN family, the Ramsays journeyed to Scotland with David I, when he went to claim his throne (1124). They may have taken their name from the image on an abbey seal (a ram in the sea), which was linked with the king. By the 13th century, they had acquired the lands of Dalhousie in Midlothian, their principal seat. William Ramsay de Dalwolsy signed the Declaration of Arbroath (1320) and his son, Alexander, was appointed Sheriff of Teviotdale in 1342. This was bitterly resented by William Douglas, who starved him to death in Hermitage Castle. Notable family members include Allan Ramsay the poet (1686–1758) and his son, also Allan (1713–1784), the portraitist.

Rankin

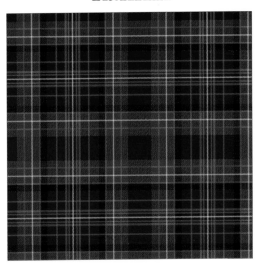

*The Rankins, who use this tartan, were followers
of the MacLeans of Coll.*

RANKIN WAS a pet form of several different forenames, including Randolph, Reginald, and Reynard. As such, it was current in many parts of Scotland, although the name appears to have been most common in Ayrshire. The Rankins were smallholders there from the 16th century. Elsewhere, John Rankyne was recorded as a burgess of Glasgow in 1456, while Peter Rankyne of the Scheild witnessed a charter in Kilmarnock (1504). Johannes Rankyn held the post of chaplain in Glasgow (1503), and William Rankine was a notary in Ayr (1590). At the same time, Rankin continued in use as a popular forename. Ranequin Kennedy, for example, served with the Scots Guards in France.

Rattray

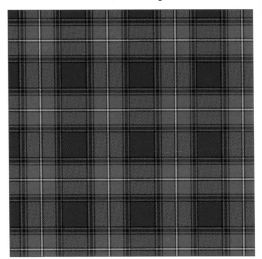

This tartan belongs to a notable Perthshire clan,
which can boast a proud, military tradition.

THIS CLAN TAKES its name from the Barony of Rattray in Perthshire or, more specifically, a rath (an ancient Pictish fort) on the estate. Alan of Rattray was documented in several 12th-century charters. His descendant, Sir Silvester Rattray, gained the post of ambassador and inherited sizeable estates at Fortingall in Atholl. In time, however, a serious feud developed with the Earls of Atholl, leading to the murder of Patrick Rattray in 1533. Eventually, the clan chose a new seat, at Craighall in Nether Kinballoch, consolidating their lands into the single Barony of Craighall-Rattray (1648).

ROBERTSON SEE PAGES **116–117**

Rollo

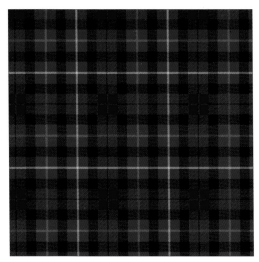

A modern tartan, designed for
Lord Rollo in 1946.

ALMOST CERTAINLY, the clan has Norman roots. The original Rollo (or Rolf) was a Viking leader, who founded the Duchy of Normandy in 911. Erik Rollo, nephew of William I, took part in the Conquest (1066) and one of his descendants travelled to Scotland with David I, when he claimed his throne (1124). The name was cited on a charter of 1141, but the first figure of note was John Rollok, secretary to the king's brother, who was granted the lands of Duncrub in 1380. For his services during the Civil War, Sir Andrew was created Lord Rollo of Duncrub in 1651, and the title of Baron Dunning was added to the family honours in 1869.

Rose

This dress tartan was recorded in 1842, but
there is an older hunting version (1831).

THE CLAN STEMS from the Norman family of de Ros, who settled in the Nairn region in the 13th century. Hugh de Ros of Geddes witnessed the foundation charter of Beauly Priory in 1219, and his son acquired the lands of Kilravock through marriage. The Roses aided Bruce during the wars against the English, capturing Invernairn Castle in 1306. Hugh, 10th Laird, was a trusted friend of Mary Queen of Scots, while the 16th Laird entertained Prince Charles on the eve of Culloden.

KILRAVOCK CASTLE *The Rose's ancestral home. Mary Queen of Scots, Bonnie Prince Charlie, and Robert Burns have all stayed as guests.*

Robertson

THE CLAN IS VERY closely linked with the Duncans. Both claimed descent from the Celtic Mormaers of Atholl, styling themselves 'de Atholia' until the 14th century. Their common ancestor was Donnachadh Reamhar ('Fat Duncan'), one of Bruce's most stalwart followers, who fought with him at Bannockburn. He had a son called Robert, who eventually became the founder of the Robertsons. Duncan, meanwhile, led the clan at Bannockburn and seems to have continued warring against the English, for he is thought to have been captured at the Battle of Neville's Cross (1346). He married twice, acquiring considerable property on each occasion. This included the

ROBERTSON HUNTING (BELOW) *This pattern was first published in Johnston's* Tartans of the Clans and Septs of Scotland *(1906).*

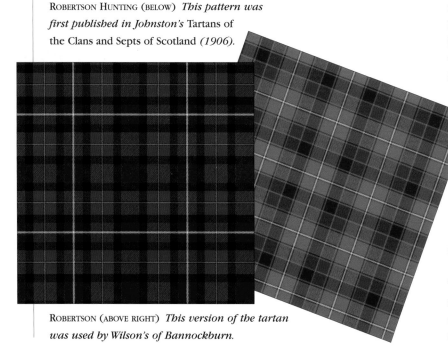

ROBERTSON (ABOVE RIGHT) *This version of the tartan was used by Wilson's of Bannockburn.*

lands of Rannoch, which would later become the seat of the Robertsons.

The standing of the clan rose considerably in the 15th century, during the chiefship of Robert Riach ('Robert the Grizzled'). In 1437, Walter, Earl of Atholl, and Sir Robert Graham led a conspiracy against James I, stabbing him to death in his lodgings at the Dominican Priory in Perth. The Queen was also wounded, trying to defend her husband. Robert Riach brought the killers to justice and, in recognition of his services, his estates were later erected into the Barony of Struan (1451). He lived on until 1460, when he was killed in a dispute over the lands of Little Dunkeld.

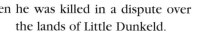

ALEXANDER ROBERTSON
Known as 'the poet chief' a volume of Alexander's poems was published after his death.

Robert's successors suffered from similar problems. William, 6th Chief, became embroiled in a feud with the Earls of Atholl, concerning the boundaries of their estates. In 1530, he was ambushed and slain by a group of the Earl's followers. Increasingly, the family fell into debt and many of their lands, heavily mortgaged, were seized by the Earl. This situation was only rectified in 1606, when John Robertson, a wealthy Edinburgh merchant, re-purchased much of the property for his kinsmen.

The clan gained a reputation as fervent supporters of the Stuarts. The first to follow this path was Donald, 'the Tutor of Struan', who acted as regent for the 12th Chief during his minority. He raised a regiment from the clan and played an active role in the campaigns of the Marquis of Montrose. His soldiers distinguished themselves at the

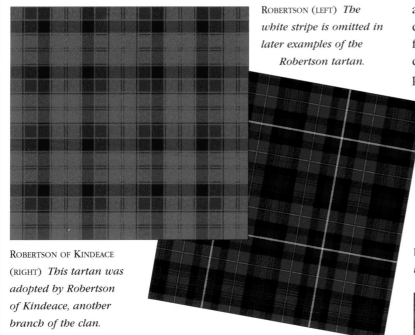

ROBERTSON (LEFT) *The white stripe is omitted in later examples of the Robertson tartan.*

ROBERTSON OF KINDEACE (RIGHT) *This tartan was adopted by Robertson of Kindeace, another branch of the clan.*

amnesty, returning to Scotland in 1726. Even so, he called out the clan during the '45 rebellion, although he was too old to take part in the fighting and suffered no reprisals. Against all the odds, he eventually died peacefully at his home in 1749. After his death, a volume of his poems was published, together with his history of the clan. Walter Scott is said to have used Alexander's remarkable life as the basis for the character of Bradwardine in *Waverley* (1814).

In addition to the Robertsons of Struan, the clan has several other branches. The oldest of these is the Robertsons of Lude, who are descended from Patrick de Atholia, the eldest son from Fat Duncan's second marriage. Other lines include the Robertsons of Kindeace, Inshes, Kinlochmoidart, and Auchleeks.

DUN ALASDAIR RESERVOIR *This takes its name from Mount Alexander (Alasdair in Gaelic), an 18th-century hermitage built by Alexander Robertson.*

Battle of Inverlochy (1645) and, in the following year, Donald was made a colonel. After the Restoration, Charles II granted him a generous pension.

Alexander, 'the poet chief', was equally committed to the cause. Born in *c.*1670, he does not appear to have fought at Killiecrankie (1689), though he shared the punishment of many of the rebels, for his lands were forfeited and he was obliged to seek refuge in France. Alexander was allowed to return to Scotland in 1703, but he never sought a formal pardon and did not hesitate to join the rising of 1715. He was taken prisoner at the Battle of Sheriffmuir, but managed to escape, only to be captured for a second time in the Highlands. The order was given to send him down to Edinburgh but, with the assistance of his sister, Alexander managed to slip away once more, this time making good his escape to France. Yet again, he was granted an

Ross

The earliest known version of this tartan is in the Cockburn Collection, Glasgow (c.1810).

Named after the province of Ross (literally 'a promontory') this clan is sometimes known in Gaelic as the Clan Andrias. This may refer to St Andrew or to a member of the O'Beolan family, who were linked to the Rosses through marriage. Either way, the accepted ancestor of the clan is Fearchar Mac an t'sagairt ('Son of the Priest'), so-called because he was descended from the hereditary abbots of Applecross. Fearchar assisted Alexander II in quelling a rebellion in the north, for which he was knighted (1215) and later created Earl of Ross (*c.*1234). The principal branches of the family are the Balnagowans, the Hawkheads, and the Shandwicks.

Russell

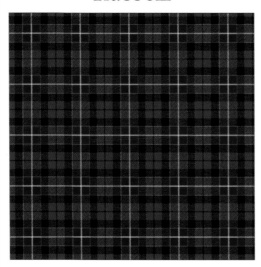

Also known as the Galbraith and Hunter, this tartan is from Wilson's pattern book (1847).

From Norman roots, the clan name may come from rous ('red') or from the hamlet of Rosel, near Caen. Several 12th-century charters bear the name of Russel and, in 1296, Robert Russel was a signatory on one of the Ragman Rolls. The north-eastern branch of the family arrived later. An Anglo-Norman baron named Rozel fought alongside Edward III at the siege of Berwick and the Battle of Halidon Hill (1333), before settling on the Aden estate in Aberdeenshire. Other members of the clan lived in Banffshire, where Patrick Russel obtained the lands of Moncoffer in 1680, and in Ashiesteel, Selkirkshire, which became the home of a soldiering branch of the family.

Ruthven

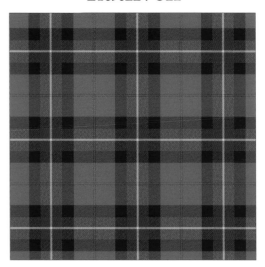

First recorded in the Vestiarium Scoticum, *published in 1842.*

The Ruthvens are said to be descended from Norse settlers. Their founder, Sweyn, donated land to the monks of Scone in 1188 and his grandson became the first to adopt the name of Ruthven, taking it from their Perthshire estates. Their later history was tainted by scandal. Patrick Ruthven was heavily implicated in the murder of Rizzio, Mary Queen of Scots' secretary, and his son, the 1st Earl of Gowrie, was executed (1584) for the abduction of James VI in the so-called 'Ruthven Raid'. Barely had the dust settled, when the family became involved in the 'Gowrie Conspiracy' (1600), which led to their name and arms being proscribed.

Scott see pages 120–121

Scrymgeour

A modern tartan, first displayed at a clan gathering at Dudhope Castle, Dundee (1971).

THE NAME COMES from an archaic word for 'skirmisher' or 'swordsman'. The family were established in Fife. Two documents of 1298 confirmed Alexander Schrymeschur's appointment as Constable of Dundee Castle and his right to act as royal standard-bearer. This was a dangerous duty and, when Alexander was captured by the English, Edward I promptly had him hanged (1306). In 1370, the Scrymgeours acquired the estates of Glassary in Argyll through marriage, adding the lands of Dudhope, Dundee, in 1495. John Scrymgeour was made Viscount Dudhope in 1641 and the 3rd Earl was rewarded with the Earldom of Dundee (1660), for his services in the Civil War.

Sempill

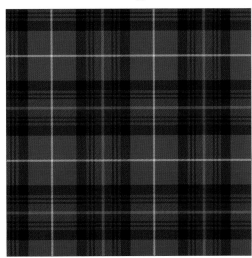

This tartan is used by a Lowland clan, closely associated with Eliotstoun in Renfrewshire.

SEMPILL IS first recorded in 1246, when Robert de Sempill was witness to a charter from Paisley Abbey. The family held the hereditary post of Sheriff of Renfrew and came into favour under Robert the Bruce. He gave them lands in Ayrshire, which had been confiscated from Balliol, and the Sempills later acquired their principal estate, Eliotstoun. They were loyal servants of the Crown – Sempill Chiefs fell at Sauchieburn (1488) and Flodden (1513) – and gained their greatest influence under the Stuarts. Lord Robert supported the cause of the infant James VI, opposed Bothwell and the Regent Morton, and was almost executed for his pains.

Seton

This design was featured in the Sobieski Stuarts' book, Vestiarium Scoticum *(1842).*

SETON LANDS may derive their name from the 'sea-town' of Tranent, close to Edinburgh, or else from the village of Sai, in Normandy. By the mid-12th century, they were in the possession of Alexander de Seton. His descendant, Sir Christopher, married Bruce's sister, acquiring further lands and influence. The Setons played a pivotal role in the career of Mary Queen of Scots. George, 5th Lord, was her Master of the Household and, after Rizzio's murder, he sheltered her in Seton Castle. He also helped her to escape from Lochleven Castle, where she was imprisoned in 1568. George's sister was one of 'the Four Marys', the Queen's loyal companions.

Scott

THE CLAN TAKES its name from the Scots, an ancient tribal people who originated in Ulster and migrated to the Scottish mainland in the early 6th century AD. There, they founded the kingdom of Dalriada, which formed the core of the future Scottish nation. The name can be traced back to the early 12th century, when Uchtredus filius Scoti (Uchtred, son of a Scot) was cited in several charters. He is thought to have had two sons. Richard, the eldest, is claimed as the ancestor of the Scotts of Buccleuch, while Michael's line produced the Scotts of Balweary.

In the following century, Sir Richard Scott married the heiress of Murthockstone, thus acquiring her lands. He was also appointed Ranger of Ettrick Forest, which brought him the estates of Rankilburn, and was the first member of the family to adopt the name Buccleuch. Sir Michael, 2nd Laird of Buccleuch, offered his services to Robert the Bruce and fought bravely at the Battle of Halidon (1333). He had two sons, the younger of whom was John, the ancestor of the Lords of Polwarth.

Robert, the 5th Laird, enlarged the family estates when he acquired a portion of the lands of Branxholm. His successor obtained the rest of this estate, in exchange for Murthockstone in Lanarkshire. Branxholm was erected into a free barony in 1463 and, by the end of the century, the Scotts had established themselves as one of the most powerful clans in the Borders. Sir Walter, 9th Laird, enhanced this position in 1551, when he was made Warden of Liddesdale and the Middle Marches. His triumph was short-lived, however, for he was murdered a year later by the Kerrs of Cessford. This was part of a long-running feud between the two families, which was ended

SIR WALTER SCOTT *Scott did much to promote the revival of interest in Scottish tartans.*

by Sir Thomas Kerr's marriage to Janet Scott, sister of the 10th Laird of Buccleuch.

The Scotts were made Lords in 1606 and Earls of Buccleuch in 1619. They subsequently acquired a dukedom through marriage. Francis, 2nd Earl, died prematurely in 1651, leaving two infant daughters. The younger of these, Anne, succeeded to the chiefship a decade later, becoming heiress to the Buccleuch fortune. She was deemed such a good catch that Charles II married her off to his illegitimate son, the Duke of Monmouth (1663), creating them Duke and Duchess of Buccleuch. Monmouth was executed in 1685, for mounting a rebellion against James VII, but the duchess was allowed to keep her title. Her grandson, Francis, became the 2nd Duke in 1732. He married Jane Douglas,

SIR WALTER SCOTT (RIGHT) *This sett was apparently designed by Scott himself in 1822. First recorded by Smibert (1850).*

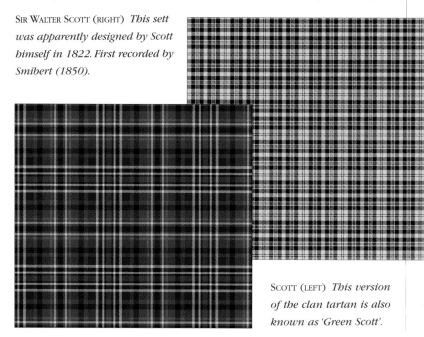

SCOTT (LEFT) *This version of the clan tartan is also known as 'Green Scott'.*

RED SCOTT *Sir Walter Scott doubted the authenticity of this design, but it is very popular today.*

the heiress of the Queensberrys, and their grandson, Henry, became the 3rd Duke of Buccleuch and 5th Duke of Queensberry. The Scotts also acquired the estate of Drumlanrig through this marriage.

Two of the most celebrated family members came from secondary branches of the clan. The man known as Michael Scot the Wizard (*c*.1175–*c*.1235) belonged to the Scotts of Balweary. Despite the supernatural overtones of his name, Scot was a respected scientist and one of the foremost intellectuals of his day. He is thought to have studied at Oxford and probably taught at the University of Paris. He translated texts from Hebrew and Arabic, introducing the West to the writings of Averroes and Avicenna and, for many years, he was both physician and court astrologer to Emperor Frederick II.

Nevertheless, it was Scot's other interests which captured the popular imagination. He studied alchemy and the occult, which gave rise to the belief that he could cast spells and conjure up demons. Dante included him among the lost souls in his *Inferno* and, it was said that he split the Eildon Hills into three and trapped a plague-demon in the crypt of Glenluce Abbey, where he starved it to death.

There was no keener student of the many legends surrounding Michael Scot than an even more distinguished member of the clan, Sir Walter Scott (1771–1832). He was descended from the Scotts of Harden through a junior branch of the Scotts of Raeburn. His great

grandfather, also called Walter, was a devoted Jacobite and fought in the 1715 uprising. He gained the nickname of 'Beardie', because he refused to shave until the Stuarts were returned to the throne.

Scott worked as an advocate and as Deputy-Sheriff of Selkirk, before turning to literature. In a series of bestselling novels – among them, *Waverley* (1814), *Rob Roy* (1817), and *The Legend of Montrose* (1819) – he re-invented Scotland's past, creating a romantic image of the country, which fascinated all of Europe. He also did much to popularize the wearing of tartan, when he stage-managed the arrangements for George IV's visit to Edinburgh. In private, though, he was conservative in his views about Highland dress. He believed that the Lowland clans had no significant tradition in this field, apart from the simple shepherd's plaid. The plainness of his personal tartan underlined this conviction.

DRUMLANRIG *This spectacular estate is now the home of the Montagu Douglas Scotts, otherwise known as the Dukes of Buccleuch and Queensberry.*

Shaw

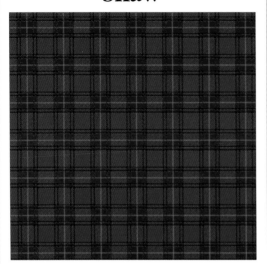

Based on the Black Watch tartan, this was
first published by McIan (c.1845).

THE ANCESTOR OF the clan is thought to be Shaw MacDuff, who was also the founder of the Mackintoshes. Indeed, the first recognised Chief of the Shaws was the second son of Angus, 6th Chief of the Mackintosh clan. Through this connection, the Shaws became part of the Clan Chattan Confederation. Shaw 'Bucktooth', 2nd Chief, was Captain of the Confederation during the Angus Raid of 1391 and the combat of champions at North Inch (1396). In 1468, his grandson, Aedh, acquired the lands of Tordarroch in Strathnairn, founding a new branch of the clan. This became known as Clan Aedh or Ay. The Shaws also held land on Harris and the Isles.

Sinclair

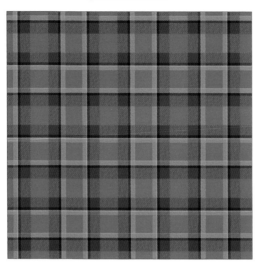

This tartan was featured in a portrait of the
13th Earl of Caithness (1790-1858).

THIS CLAN HAS Norman roots, taking its name from the French parish of St Clair. Walderne de Sancto Claro took part in the Conquest and his descendant, William, was granted the Barony of Roslin, near Edinburgh. Henry St Clair gained the Earldom of Orkney (1379), annexed the Faroes (1391), and discovered Greenland. Some even claim that he voyaged as far as the Americas. Orkney was later ceded to the Crown, but the Sinclairs became Earls of Caithness (1455). More recently, Sir John Sinclair of Ulbster (1754-1835) founded the British Wool Society, rebuilt Thurso, and wrote pamphlets on Highland dress.

Skene

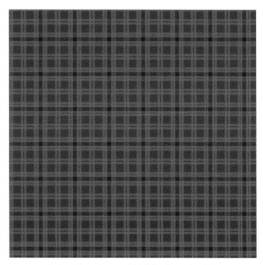

Published by Grant (1886), but similar to a
version in Wilson's pattern book (1830).

A YOUNGER SON of Robertson of Struan is claimed as the founder of this clan. By tradition, he rescued the king from a murderous wolf by killing it with his small knife (*sgian-dubh*). In recompense, he was given an estate near Aberdeen, naming it after the sgian, the instrument of his good fortune. John de Skeen lost his lands after opposing King Edgar, but they were restored (1118) under Alexander I. Patrick de Skene was a signatory of the Ragman Rolls, but his successors were keen supporters of the Scottish Crown, sacrificing their lives at the battles of Harlaw, Flodden, and Pinkie. After 1827, when the direct line died out, the chiefship passed to the Skenes of Halyards.

Spens

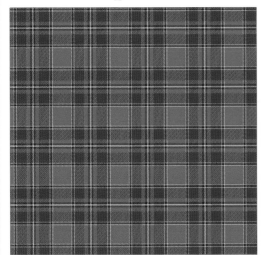

*Versions of the Spens' tartan were noted by
Wilson's and the Highland Society (early 1900s).*

THE NAME probably comes from the post of dispensator, a type of steward in ecclesiastical or secular households. Roger 'the Dispensator' was cited in a deed of 1232. According to one of the most famous Border Ballads, Sir Patrick Spens died at sea in 1281, after escorting Princess Margaret to her marriage in Norway. Then, in the 15th century, Thomas Spens rose to become Lord Privy Seal and Bishop of Aberdeen, while his brother, Patrick, joined the Garde Ecossaise, the bodyguard of the French king. Dr Nathaniel Spens was the subject of one of Raeburn's finest tartan portraits (1792).

STEWART SEE PAGES 124–129

Stirling

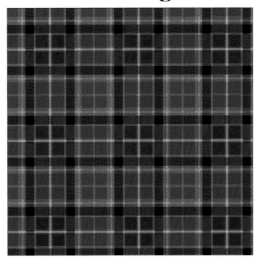

*This is a district tartan for Stirling and
Bannockburn, produced by Wilson's (c.1847).*

THIS CLAN TAKES its name from the town of Stirling (literally 'place of strife'), which is closely associated with William Wallace and Scotland's struggle for freedom. The family traces its line back to Thoraldus, holder of the lands of Cadder in 1147. One of his descendants, Sir Alexander de Strivelyn (d.1304), 5th Laird of Cadder, was the first to adopt the name. Sir John de Strivelyn became James I's armour bearer and the Governor of Dumbarton Castle, a post that was also held by his successors. The Stirlings of Glenesk were the original owners of Edzell Castle in Angus, while another branch of the family gained the lands of Keir, in Perthshire.

Sturrock

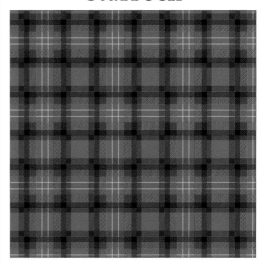

*A sample from the MacGregor-Hastie
Collection, dating from the 1930s.*

LITTLE IS KNOWN about the origins of this family, although they seem to have been numerous in the rural parts of Angus. Their name, which can also take the form of Storach or Storek, has been variously interpreted as a 'sheep farmer' or a 'store-master' (a farmer). The earliest records date from the 15th century, when Laurentius Sturrok was a chaplain in Aberdeen (1448), later becoming vicar of the parish church at Covil (1453). By contrast, John Storrock of Dundee was taken into custody for being a 'schismatik and a disorderly person' (1676).

Stewart

THE STEWART HISTORY is exciting and well-documented, and makes this clan probably one of the best known Scottish names. Many family members were involved in the struggle for the Scottish crown, including Mary Queen of Scots and Bonnie Prince Charlie, and the history of this dynasty is a history of Great Britain as well as Scotland. The Royal Stewart tartan has always been regarded as the tartan of the royal house of Scotland, and is now also the royal tartan of Her Majesty the Queen.

There used to be a legend that the Stewarts were descended from Banquo, the murdered thane in Shakespeare's *Macbeth*. It is now accepted, however, that their forebears were Norman. Their ancestor was Alain, Seneschal of Dol in Brittany. He joined the First Crusade in 1097, but his successors settled in Scotland during the reign of David I (1124–1153). One of these, Walter, became High Steward of the royal household, a hereditary post which gave the clan its name.

Walter was granted land in Renfrew and Paisley, and took part in the successful campaign against Somerled of the Isles (1164). James, 5th High Steward, supported Wallace and Bruce in the wars against England, while Walter, 6th High Steward, married Bruce's daughter, Marjory. In due course, this match brought the Stewarts the crown for, when David II died childless,

Marjory's son ascended the throne as Robert II (1371). After this, the Stewarts ruled Scotland for more than three hundred years.

In addition to their royal line, the clan had several important offshoots. The most notable of these was the Stewarts of Appin, who were descended from Sir John Stewart of Bonkyl (d.1298), son of the 4th High Steward. His younger son, James, was killed at the Battle of Halidon (1333) and his grandson became the 1st Stewart Lord of Lorne. The family acquired Appin itself in the following century and Duncan, 2nd of Appin, held the post of Chamberlain of the Isles and built Castle Stalker.

Another branch, the Stewarts of Atholl, also stemmed from the 4th High Steward. One of his descendants, Sir John Stewart of Balveny was made 5th Earl of Atholl by his half-brother, James II. Sir John had no son, however, so the title passed to the Murrays. The Stuarts of Bute, meanwhile, were descended from 'Black Stewart', an illegitimate son of Robert II.

The destiny of the house of Stewart underwent a dramatic transformation during the middle years of the 16th century. As the country's political fortunes shifted rapidly, its leaders faced a daunting prospect: they might soon

BONNIE PRINCE CHARLIE

Also known as the Young Pretender, Prince Charles Edward was the grandson of the last Stuart king, James VII.

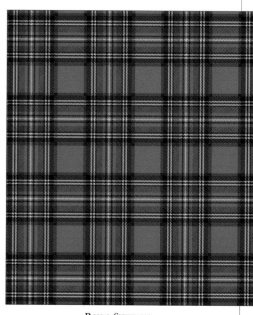

ROYAL STEWART

In use since the 18th century, this is the tartan worn by Her Majesty the Queen.

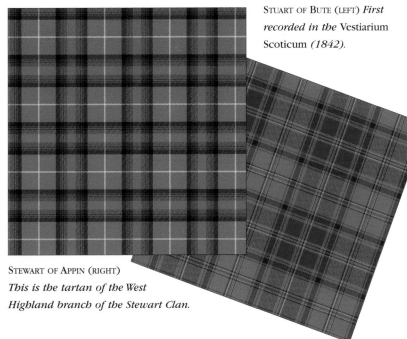

STUART OF BUTE (LEFT) *First recorded in the* Vestiarium Scoticum *(1842).*

STEWART OF APPIN (RIGHT)
This is the tartan of the West Highland branch of the Stewart Clan.

Moss, and his baby girl was barely one week old. Nevertheless, problems did not arise instantly. After the king's death, the regency was assumed by James Stewart, 2nd Earl of Arran, and Mary was sheltered in a succession of secure strongholds. These included Inchmahome Island, Stirling Castle, and Dumbarton Rock. The long-term difficulty, however, lay with the question of marriage, for the child's lineage offered potential suitors a dangerously tempting royal prize.

The first contender was Henry VIII, who wanted Mary to marry his son Edward and launched punitive raids into the Lowlands, to try and force the issue. With characteristically dry humour, the Scots referred to this as 'the Rough Wooing'. Instead, the Queen was married off to the young dauphin, who ascended the French throne as François II in 1559. François ruled for just one year but, even in this

unite three royal thrones – the kingdoms of England, France, and Scotland – or else be left with nothing.

Two minor incidents hinted at future developments. In 1537, the Earl of Lennox adopted French nationality and decided to spell his name 'Stuart', since this was easier for his new companions to pronounce. Gradually, this version began to replace the more familiar, Scottish spelling. Then, five years later, as James V lay on his deathbed, he uttered his gloomy prophecy on the fate of the Stewarts: 'It came with a lass and it will gang with a lass'. By this, he meant the Scottish throne, for it had come into Stewart hands through Margery Bruce and it seemed likely that it would be lost by his own daughter, Mary Queen of Scots.

James's pessimism was understandable. He had just undertaken an abortive invasion of England, which had ended in defeat at Solway

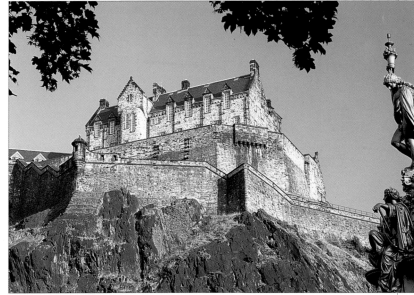

EDINBURGH CASTLE *James VI was born here in June 1566. In the museum, the Appin colours are displayed – the only Jacobite banner to survive from Culloden.*

short time, his threat to the English Crown was all too apparent. For French Catholics did not recognize Henry VIII's divorce and thus regarded his daughter Elizabeth – the new Queen of England – as illegitimate. Accordingly, they believed that Mary had a better claim to the English throne through her grandmother, Margaret Tudor, Henry VIII's sister. Ultimately, this accident of birth would lead to the downfall of the Scottish queen.

Mary's situation was aggravated by her own marital problems. After François' death, she married her cousin, Henry Stuart, Lord Darnley (1565). Had this marriage survived, the Stewart fortunes would have been greatly enhanced. Instead, Darnley killed the Queen's secretary, Rizzio, in a fit of jealousy and was in turn murdered

STEWART OF ATHOLL (LEFT) *Clansmen are said to have worn this tartan during the '45 rebellion.*

STEWART BLACK (ABOVE) *There was a sample of this tartan in Paton's collection which was assembled in the 1830s.*

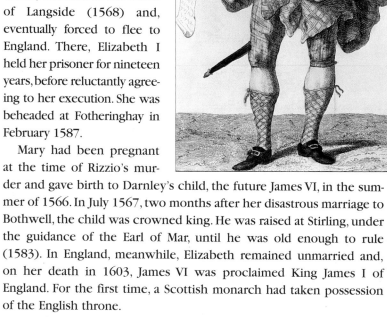

WANTED POSTER (RIGHT) *For five months after Culloden, Bonnie Prince Charlie was a fugitive in the Highlands, with a reward of £30,000 on his head.*

by her new favourite, the Earl of Bothwell. Mary's marriage to the latter in 1567 unleashed a storm of protest, as her countrymen turned against her. She was imprisoned for a time at Loch Leven Castle, defeated at the Battle of Langside (1568) and, eventually forced to flee to England. There, Elizabeth I held her prisoner for nineteen years, before reluctantly agreeing to her execution. She was beheaded at Fotheringhay in February 1587.

Mary had been pregnant at the time of Rizzio's murder and gave birth to Darnley's child, the future James VI, in the summer of 1566. In July 1567, two months after her disastrous marriage to Bothwell, the child was crowned king. He was raised at Stirling, under the guidance of the Earl of Mar, until he was old enough to rule (1583). In England, meanwhile, Elizabeth remained unmarried and, on her death in 1603, James VI was proclaimed King James I of England. For the first time, a Scottish monarch had taken possession of the English throne.

For almost a century, the government of the two kingdoms ran in tandem. James VI ruled until 1625, when he was succeeded by his son,

STEWART DRESS *Along with the Royal Stewart, this tartan is known throughout the world as a symbol of Scotland.*

Charles I. His reign was marred by the Civil War (1642-1649), which ended with his execution. In Scotland, opposition to Charles' religious policies was upheld by the Covenanters. Their principles were enshrined in two documents – the National Covenant (1638) and the Solemn League and Covenant (1643). Charles eventually surrendered to the Scottish army at Newark (1646) and was handed over to the English for trial. His son, Charles II, was restored to the throne in 1660, but James VII (James II of England) was the last of the undisputed Stuart monarchs. In England, he ruled for just three years (1685-1688), before being deposed for his Catholic sympathies.

The accession of a Protestant, William of Orange, was broadly popular in Scotland, but James could still command some support from the Jacobites (from *Jacobus*, Latin for 'James'). They won a victory at Killiecrankie (1689), but were unable to press home their advantage. Even so, resentment of King William increased dramatically in 1692, when it appeared that he had instigated the Massacre of Glencoe, as a means of suppressing opposition in the Highlands. As a result, many of the Scottish clans warmed to the idea of a Stuart revival. This was evident to William III's successor, Queen Anne (1702-1714). Fearing that the Scots might choose their own king, she quickly brought the Treaty of Union into force (1707). The Jacobites, of course, did not accept this. James VII had died in 1701, but his exiled heirs were known to Stuart supporters as 'the Kings over the Water'. The first to bear this 'title' was Prince James Francis Edward, James VII's son. In 1701, he was recognized by the French king as 'James VIII', although he became better known by his nickname, 'the Old Pretender'.

The first Jacobite uprising took place in 1715. In Scotland, a group of nobles, led by John Erskine, 6th Earl of Mar, raised an army of

MARY QUEEN OF SCOTS' BED *This bed was originally at Terreagles House but is now in the King's room at Traquair. It is said to be the one in which Mary Queen of Scots spent her last night in Scotland before fleeing to England to seek help from her cousin Queen Elizabeth I.*

Highlanders and proclaimed James as their king. Some of these captured Perth and marched south, where they were defeated at Preston, while another force fought an inconclusive battle at Sheriffmuir. All this took place while James was still in France. He arrived in Scotland only in December 1715, more than three months after the rebellion had been launched. It was already too late. By this stage, Mar's army was beginning to melt away and the Prince fled ignominiously back to France in February 1716.

In 1719, James made another, even less auspicious attempt to capture the throne, this time with Spanish support. After its failure, he retired to Rome and it was left to his eldest son, Prince Charles Edward, to take up the Jacobite cause. Because of his considerable personal magnetism, he was dubbed 'Bonnie Prince Charlie' (also the 'Young Pretender').

STEWART HUNTING *The earliest known record of this sett was in the pattern books of Wilson's, the regimental weavers from Bannockburn (1819).*

Originally, the second Jacobite rising was due to take place with French backing. In 1744, an invasion fleet gathered at Dunkirk, but this was dispersed by a violent storm and the scheme had to be abandoned. Charles' French allies showed no signs of making a further attempt, so the Prince pawned his jewels, borrowed some money and set off alone. In July 1745, he landed at Eriskay in the Outer Hebrides, accompanied by just seven men – the so-called 'Seven Men of Moidart'. After reaching the mainland, however, Charles gained the support of two influential clan chiefs – MacDonald of Clanranald and Cameron of Lochiel. With their backing, he felt confident enough to raise the royal standard at Glenfinnan on 19 August 1745, proclaiming his father king.

Initially, the campaign went well. Perth and Edinburgh were soon secured and a notable victory was achieved at Prestonpans. By this stage, more Highland clans had joined the cause, among them the Macphersons, the Stewarts of Appin, the Robertsons, and the men of Atholl. So, with an army of around 8,000, Charlie began the march south, hoping that his ranks would be swelled by discontented Catholics and support from France. In the event, neither of these materialized and the Jacobites reached only Derby, before starting to retreat northwards. They won a skirmish at Falkirk in January 1746,

TRAQUAIR *This has been in Stuart hands since 1491, when the Earl of Buchan bestowed it on James Stuart, the 1st Laird.*

but the English army, led by the Duke of Cumberland, was biding its time until the end of winter. It was April before the decisive conflict took place, at Culloden Moor near Inverness.

The battle was very one-sided, lasting less than an hour. Cumberland's artillery decimated the Scots and Charles was forced to flee. For five months, he roamed the Highlands with a price on his head. To their credit, none of his countrymen tried to claim this, although he was an embarrassment and a liability to many of his hosts. Eventually, however, with the aid of Flora MacDonald, he made his way to Skye and escaped on a French brig, ironically called *L'Heureux* ('the fortunate one').

The repercussions of defeat were horrendous for the Scots. More than a hundred of the high-ranking prisoners were executed; over a thousand clansmen were deprived of their lands and deported; and the Government did their best to extinguish all traces of Highland culture, banning both the kilt and the pipes.

The last years of the Stuarts were something of an anti-climax. The Old Pretender continued to live in Rome, until his death in 1766. Prince Charles remained in Paris until 1748, when the French king was obliged to make him leave. Two years later, he made a secret visit to England, where it became clear that the Jacobite cause was defunct. In later life, he took to drink, suffering an unhappy love affair

with Clementina Walkinshaw and an even unhappier marriage with Princess Louise of Stolberg. He died in Rome in 1788.

Prince Charles' younger brother, Henry, also had a technical claim to the throne, but he was realistic enough to ignore it. In 1747, he was made Cardinal York. He, too, spent his final years in Rome, living on a pension provided by the English king, George III. A single tomb in St. Peter's marks the resting place of all three 'kings over the water'.

ROYAL STEWART *This print from Robert McIan's* The Clans of the Scottish Highlands (1845) *illustrates the Royal Stewart tartan.*

CASTLE STALKER *Built in the mid-16th century, this was a stronghold of the Stewarts of Appin, until their lands were forfeited after Culloden.*

Sutherland

A letter of 1618 describes this sett, though it was first illustrated in 1842.

THE NAME ('South Land') indicates that this was the southernmost territory of the Norse chieftains, who also held Orkney, Shetland, and Caithness. The family itself derives from Freskin, who was also the ancestor of the Murrays. He may have been Pictish, though it is more likely that he was a Flemish mercenary, employed by the Normans. In *c*.1130, the family was granted land in Duffus and Moray, gaining the title of Earl of Sutherland a century later. This is said to be the oldest earldom in Britain.

DUNROBIN CASTLE *The Sutherlands have owned this magnificent pile since the 13th century, making it one of Scotland's oldest inhabited castles.*

Taylor

Designed by Iain Cameron Taylor, this resembles the Cameron tartan in Vestiarium Scoticum.

As WITH MOST names relating to trades or professions, Taylors were widely dispersed throughout Scotland. Alexander le Taillur was listed as a royal valet in 1276 while, twenty years later, Bryce le Taillur was among those taken by the English at Dunbar Castle. No fewer than six Taylors signed the Ragman Rolls, though the name was spelt in a variety of ways. In 1613, members of the Macintaileour family were arrested for harbouring outlawed MacGregors. There were also very close links with the Cameron clan. Taillear Dubh na Tuaighe (Black Taylor of the Axe) was a much-feared, 17th-century warrior, whose descendants often bore the name Cameron Taylor.

Urquhart

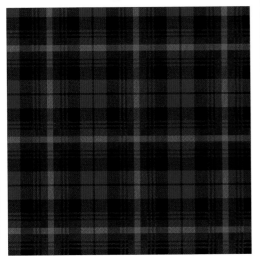

The earliest version of the tartan (c.1810) comes from the Cockburn Collection, Glasgow.

THE CLAN TAKES its name from the district of Urquhart in the former county of Cromarty, where the family held the hereditary post of sheriff. It rose to prominence in the 14th century, when William Urquhart married the daughter of the powerful Earl of Ross, but its most famous member was the Cavalier author, Sir Thomas Urquhart (c.1611-1660). In addition to his literary works, he produced a spurious genealogy of the family, tracing their descent back to Adam and Eve.

URQUHART CASTLE *Once a Comyn stronghold, this castle on Loch Ness was suprisingly held only briefly by the Urquharts.*

Wallace

This tartan was first recorded in the Vestiarium Scoticum, *published in 1842.*

THE NAME Wallace derives from the Latin term 'Wallensis', which normally means Welsh. In this case, however, it denotes the Britons of Strathclyde, who came from the same racial stock. The family can be traced back to Richard Wallace of Riccarton, who owned land in Ayrshire in the 12th century. He was the great-great-grandfather of William Wallace (1274-1305), who won a resounding victory against the English at Stirling Bridge in 1297. After this, Wallace was hunted down and captured; tried for treason; and then hanged, drawn, and quartered. As a final indignity, his head was put on public display at London Bridge.

Weir

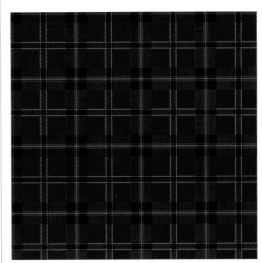

This tartan belongs to the Weirs a family named after the town of Vere in France.

ONE OF THE smaller Scottish clans, the Weirs can lay claim to great antiquity. The earliest mention of the family occurred in 1174, when Radulphus de Ver was listed as one of the lords who accompanied William the Lion on his disastrous invasion of England. Like the Scottish king, de Ver was taken prisoner at Alnwick. After this, the fortunes of the Weirs were sparsely documented until the 15th century when they held land at Lesmahagow in Lanarkshire. Then, in 1670, Major Thomas Weir and his sister were tried in Edinburgh for the crime of practising witchcraft. In due course, they were found guilty and burned at the stake.

Wemyss

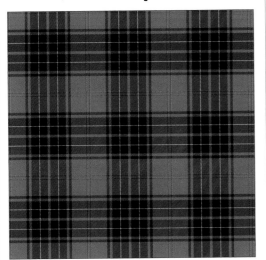

This sett was first illustrated in the Vestiarium
Scoticum, *published in 1842.*

THE NAME derives from the Gaelic word for 'cave' (*uaimb*), a reference to the many caves in the cliff-face near Wemyss Castle. The family itself claims descent from the MacDuffs, the ancient Thanes of Fife. In 1290, Sir Michael Wemyss was among the party, sent to fetch the tragic Maid of Norway and, six years later, he put his name to Edward I's Ragman Rolls. Sir John Wemyss was a supporter of Queen Mary, becoming Lieutenant of Fife, and his great-grandson was made an earl in 1633.

WEMYSS CASTLE *The main tower dates from the 14th century. Mary Queen of Scots was a guest here, when she met her future husband, Lord Darnley.*

Wilson

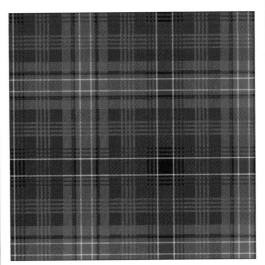

*Appropriately enough, this tartan was first made
by Wilson's of Bannockburn in c.1780.*

CHIEFLY ASSOCIATED with the Gunn and Innes clans, Wilson means 'Son of Will' (William) and it can also be found as Wolson and Wulsone. The earliest references date from the 15th century, when John Wulson was a merchant in the service of Sir John of Mountgomery (1405). Alexander Wilson (1766-1813) was born in Paisley and began his career as an itinerant poet and muslin pedlar. In Pennsylvania, however, he gained fame for his seven-volume study of American ornithology. James Wilson (1742-1798), emigrated from his native St. Andrews to become an American patriot. He signed the Declaration of Independence and helped draft the Pennsylvania Constitution.

Wotherspoon

*This sett was produced by Andersons in 1947 and
included in the MacGregor-Hastie Collection.*

ALTHOUGH TENTATIVELY interpreted as a 'sheep pasture', the meaning of this name is uncertain. It can also be written as Witherspoon or Wetherspoon. The family were established in the Lowlands by the 13th century, when Roger Wythirspon witnessed a grant of lands in Renfrewshire. The name can be found in a number of other charters, such as one endorsed by John Wyddirspwn of Dalbeth in 1518, but the first figure of note was the Reverend John Witherspoon (1722-1794). He was born in Yester, East Lothian, and became President of the College of New Jersey (now Princeton) in 1768. He later fought for his adopted country in the American War of Independence.

Families and Associated Clans

Here, we have listed some common Scottish surnames along with the clan they are usually associated with. The debate surrounding these associations still continues and so this list does not claim to be definitive.

ABBOT, ABBOTSON	MacNab
ABERNETHY	Leslie
ADAM	Gordon
ADAMSON	Mackintosh
ADIE	Gordon
AIRLIE	Ogilvie
AICHESON	Gordon
AITKEN	Gordon
ALEXANDER	MacAlister, MacDonald, MacDonell
ALLAN, ALLANSON	MacDonald, MacFarlane
ALLARDICE	Graham
ALPIN	MacAlpine
ANDREW	Ross
ARTHUR	MacArthur
AUSTIN	Keith
AYSON	Mackintosh
BAIN	MacBain, MacKay, MacNab
BANNERMAN	Forbes
BARRIE	Farquharson, Gordon
BARRON	Rose
BARTHOLOMEW	MacFarlane
BAYNE	MacBain, MacKay, MacNab
BEAN	MacBain
BEATON, BETON	MacDonald, MacLean of Duart, MacLeod
BEATTIE	MacBain
BEGG	MacDonald
BELL	Macmillan
BERKELEY	Barclay
BERRY	Forbes
BINNIE	MacBain

BLACK	Lamont, MacGregor, MacLean of Duart
BLAIR	Graham
BLAKE	Lamont
BONTEIN, BONTINE, BUNTEN	Graham
BOWERS	MacGregor
BOWMAN	Farquharson
BREBNER	Farquharson
BREWER	Drummond, MacGregor
BROWN	Lamont, Macmillan
BRYCE	MacFarlane
BURDON	Lamont
BURKE	MacDonald
CADDELL	Campbell
CAIRD	MacGregor, Sinclair
CALDER	Campbell
CALLUM	MacLeod, Campbell, MacArthur
CARISTON	Skene
CARLYLE	Bruce
CARSON	Macpherson
CATTANACH	Macpherson
CAW	MacFarlane
CHALMERS	Cameron
CHARLES	Mackenzie
CHEYNE	Sutherland
CLARKSON	Cameron, Mackintosh, Macpherson
CLUNY	Macpherson
CLYNE	Sinclair
COLLIER	Robertson
COLMAN	Buchanan
COLSON	MacDonald
COLYEAR	Robertson
COMRIE	MacGregor

CONACHER	MacDougall
CONSTABLE	Hay
COOK	Stewart
CORMACK	Buchanan
COULSON	MacDonald
COUTTS	Farquarson
COWAN	Colquhoun, MacDougall
CRERAR	Mackintosh
CROMAR	Farquharson
CROMBIE	MacDonald
CROOKSHANKS, CRUIKSHANKS	Stewart
CURRIE	MacDonald, Macpherson
DALLAS	Mackintosh
DANIELS	MacDonald
DARROCH	MacDonald
DAVIE	Davidson
DAVIS, DAVISON	Davidson
DAWSON	Davidson
DAY	Davidson
DEAN	Davidson
DENOON	Campbell
DEUCHAR	Lindsay
DEWAR	MacNab, Menzies
DICKSON	Keith
DIS, DISE	Skene
DOCHARTY	MacGregor
DOIG	Drummond
DOLES	Mackintosh
DONACHIE	Robertson
DONALD, DONALDSON	MacDonald
DONLEAVY	Buchanan
DOUGALL	MacDougall
DOVE	Buchanan
DOW	Buchanan, Davidson
DOWALL, DOWELL	MacDougall
DRYSDALE	Douglas
DUFF	MacDuff
DUFFIE, DUFFY	MacFie
DUNCANSON	Duncan

DUNNACHIE	Robertson
EADIE, EDIE	Gordon
EATON	Home
ELDER	Mackintosh
EWAN, EWEN	MacEwen
EWING	MacEwen
FAIR	Ross
FARQUHAR	Farquharson
FEDERITH	Sutherland
FERGUS	Ferguson
FERSON	Macpherson
FIFE	MacDuff
FINDLAY, FINLAY	Farquharson
FINDLAYSON, FINLAYSON	Farquharson
FINDLATER	Ogilvie
FLEMING	Murray
FORDYCE	Forbes
FOULIS	Munro
FRANCE	Stewart
FRESELL, FRISEAL, FRIZELL	Fraser
FREW	Fraser
FULLARTON	Stewart
FYFE	MacDuff
GALLIE	Gunn
GARROW	Stewart
GAUNSON	Gunn
GEDDES	Gordon
GEORGESON	Gunn
GIBB	Buchanan
GIBSON	Buchanan
GILBERT, GILBERTSON	Buchanan
GILBRIDE	MacDonald
GILCHRIST	MacLachlan, Ogilvie
GILFILLAN	MacNab
GILLANDERS	Ross
GILLESPIE	Macpherson
GILMORE	Morrison
GILROY	Grant, MacGillivray
GLEN, GLENNIE	Mackintosh
GOWRIE	MacDonald
GRACIE	Farquharson

GRAY Stewart, Sutherland
GREENLAW Home
GREGOR, GREGORSON MacGregor
GREGORY MacGregor
GREIG MacGregor
GREUSACH Farquharson
GRIER, GRIERSON MacGregor
HAGGART Ross
HALLYARD Skene
HANNA, HANNAH Hannay
HARDIE, HARDY Farquharson, Mackintosh
HARPER, HARPERSON Buchanan
HARVEY Keith
HASTINGS Campbell
HAWTHORN MacDonald
HENDRIE, HENDRY Henderson, MacNaughton
HOUSTON MacDonald
HOWE Graham
HUGHSON MacDonald
HUNTLY Gordon
HUTCHESON, HUTCHINSON MacDonald
INCHES Robertson
INGRAM Colquhoun
INNIE Innes
JAMESON Gunn, Stewart
KAY Davidson
KEAN, KEENE Gunn, MacDonald
KELLIE, KELLY MacDonald
KENDRICK Henderson, MacNaughton
KENNETH, KENNETHSON Mackenzie
KERRACHER Farquharson
KILPATRICK Colquhoun
KINNELL MacDonald
KIRKPATRICK Colquhoun
LACHLAN MacLachlan
LAMB Lamont
LAMMOND Lamont
LAMONDSON Lamont
LAURENCE, LAWRENCE MacLaren
LAW, LAWRIE MacLaren
LEAN MacLean of Duart

LECKIE, LECKY MacGregor
LEES Macpherson
LENNIE, LENNY Buchanan
LEWIS MacLeod
LIMOND, LIMONT Lamont
LOBBAN Logan
LOCKERBIE Douglas
LOMBARD Stewart
LOUDOUN Campbell
LOVE Mackinnon
LOW MacLaren
LUCAS Lamont
LYALL Sinclair
MACADAM MacGregor
MACAINDRA MacFarlane
MACALASTER MacAlister
MACALDUIE Lamont
MACALLAN MacDonald, MacFarlane
MACENDEOIR Buchanan, MacNab, Menzies
MACANDREW Mackintosh
MACANGUS MacInnes
MACARA MacGregor, MacRae
MACAREE MacGregor
MACASKILL MacLeod
MACAUSLAN, MACAUSLAND Buchanan
MACBAXTER Macmillan
MACBEATH MacBain, MacDonald, MacLean of Duart
MACBEOLAIN Mackenzie
MACBRAYNE MacNaughton
MACBRIDE MacDonald
MACBRIEVE Morrison
MACCAA MacFarlane
MACCAIG Farquharson, MacLeod
MACCAINSH MacInnes
MACCAISHE MacDonald
MACCALL MacColl
MACCALMAN Buchanan
MACCALMONT Buchanan
MACCAMIE Stewart
MACCAMMON, MACCAMMOND Buchanan
MACCANSH MacInnes

MACCARDNEY Farquharson, Mackintosh
MACCARTAIR MacArthur
MACCARTNEY Farquharson, Mackintosh
MACCASH MacDonald
MACCASKILL MacLeod
MACCAUL MacDonald
MACCAUSE MacFarlane
MACCAW Stewart
MACCAY MacKay
MACCEALLAICH MacDonald
MACCHOITER MacGregor
MACCHRUITER Buchanan
MACCLAMROCH MacKay
MACCLERICH, MACCHLERY Cameron, Mackintosh, Macpherson
MACCLOY Stewart
MACCLURE MacLeod
MACCLYMONT Lamont
MACCODRUM MacDonald
MACCOLMAN Buchanan
MACCOMAS Gunn
MACCOMBE Mackintosh
MACCOMBICH Stewart
MACCOMBIE Mackintosh
MACCONACHER MacDougall
MACCONACHIE MacGregor, Robertson
MACCONDY MacFarlane
MACCONNACH Mackenzie
MACCONNECHY Campbell, Robertson
MACCONNELL MacDonald
MACCONNICHIE Campbell, MacGregor, Robertson
MACCOOISH MacDonald
MACCOOK MacDonald
MACCORKILL, MACCORKLE Gunn
MACCORKINDALE MacLeod
MACCORMACK Buchanan, MacLaine of Lochbuie
MACCORMICK Buchanan, MacLaine of Lochbuie
MACCORQUODALE MacLeod

MACCORRIE, MACCORRY MacQuarrie
MACCOULL MacDougall
MACCOWAN Colquhoun, MacDougall
MACCRACKEN MacLean of Duart
MACCRAE, MACCREA MacRae
MACCRAIN MacDonald
MACCRAW MacRae
MACCREATH MacRae
MACCRIMMON MacLeod
MACCROWTHER MacGregor
MACCUAG MacDonald
MACCUAIG Farquharson, MacLeod
MACCUBBIN Buchanan
MACCUISH MacDonald
MACCULLOCH MacDonald, MacDougall, Munro, Ross
MACCUTCHEN, MACCUTCHEON MacDonald
MACDAID Davidson
MACDANIELL MacDonald
MACDAVID Davidson
MACDERMID Campbell
MACDONACHIE Robertson
MACDONLEAVY Buchanan
MACDOWALL, MACDOWELL MacDougall
MACDRAIN MacDonald
MACDUFFIE MacFie
MACEACHAN MacDonald
MACEACHERN, MACEACHERAN MacDonald
MACEARACHER Farquharson
MACELFRISH MacDonald
MACELHERAN MacDonald
MACERRACHER Farquharson, MacFarlane
MACFARQUHAR Farquharson
MACFATER MacLaren
MACFEAT MacLaren
MACFERGUS Ferguson
MACGAW MacFarlane

MACGEACHIE MacDonald	
MACGEOCH MacFarlane	
MACGHEE, MACGHIE MacKay	
MACGIBBON Buchanan, Campbell, Graham	
MACGILBERT Buchanan	
MACGILCHRIST MacLachlan, Ogilvie	
MACGILLEGOWIE Lamont	
MACGILLIVANTIC MacDonell	
MACGILLONIE Cameron	
MACGILP MacDonell	
MACGILROY Grant, MacGillivray	
MACGILVERNOCK Graham	
MACGORRIE, MACGORRY MacDonald, MacQuarrie	
MACGOWAN, MACGOWN MacDonald, Macpherson	
MACGRATH MacRae	
MACGREUSICH Buchanan, MacFarlane	
MACGRIME Graham	
MACGRORY MacLaren	
MACGROWTHER MacGregor	
MACGRUDER MacGregor	
MACGRUER Fraser	
MACGRUTHER MacGregor	
MACGUAIG Farquharson	
MACGUARAN MacQuarrie	
MACGUFFIE MacFie	
MACGUGAN MacDougall, MacNeil	
MACGUIRE MacQuarrie	
MACHAFFIE MacFie	
MACHAROLD MacLeod	
MACHAY Mackintosh	
MACHENDRIE, MACHENDRY Henderson, MacNaughton	
MACHOWELL MacDougall	
MACHUGH MacDonald	
MACHUTCHEN, MACHUTCHEON MacDonald	
MACILDOWIE Cameron	
MACILREACH MacDonald	
MACILREVIE MacDonald	
MACILRIACH MacDonald	

MACILROY MacGillivray, Grant	
MACILVAIN MacBain	
MACILVORA MacLaine of Lochbuie	
MACILVRAIE MacGillivray	
MACILVRIDE MacDonald	
MACILWRAITH MacDonald	
MACIMMEY Fraser	
MACINALLY Buchanan	
MACINDEOR Buchanan, MacNab, Menzies	
MACINDOE Buchanan	
MACINSTALKER MacFarlane	
MACISAAC Campbell, MacDonald	
MACJAMES MacFarlane	
MACKAIL Cameron	
MACKAMES Gunn	
MACKEACHAN MacDonald	
MACKEAMISH Gunn	
MACKEAN Gunn, MacDonald	
MACKECHNIE MacDonald	
MACKEE MacKay	
MACKEGGIE Mackintosh	
MACKEITH Keith, Macpherson	
MACKELLACHIE MacDonald	
MACKELLAIG, MACKELLAIGH MacDonald	
MACKELLAR Campbell	
MACKELLOCH MacDonald	
MACKEMMIE Fraser	
MACKENDRICK, MACKENRICK MacNaughton	
MACKEOCHAN MacDonald	
MACKERCHAR Farquharson	
MACKERLICH Mackenzie	
MACKERRACHAR Farquharson	
MACKERRAS Ferguson	
MACKERSEY Ferguson	
MACKESSOCK Campbell, MacDonald	
MACKICHAN MacDonald, MacDougall	
MACKIE MacKay	
MACKILLICAN Mackintosh	
MACKILLOP MacDonell	
MACKIM Fraser	
MACKIMMIE Fraser	
MACKINDLAY Farquharson	

MACKINNELL MacDonald	
MACKINNEY Mackinnon	
MACKINNING Mackinnon	
MACKINVEN Mackinnon	
MACKISSOCK Campbell, MacDonald	
MACKNIGHT MacNaughton	
MACLAGAN Robertson	
MACLAGHLAN MacLachlan	
MACLAMOND MacLachlan	
MACLARDIE, MACLARDY MacDonald	
MACLARTY MacDonald	
MACLAVERTY MacDonald	
MACLEISH Macpherson	
MACLELLAN MacDonald	
MACLERGAIN MacLean of Duart	
MACLERIE Cameron, Mackintosh, Macpherson	
MACLEWIS MacLeod, Stewart	
MACLISE Macpherson	
MACLIVER MacGregor	
MACLUCAS Lamont, MacDougall	
MACLUGASH MacDougall	
MACLULICH MacDougall, Munro, Ross	
MACLURE MacLeod	
MACLYMONT Lamont	
MACMANUS Colquhoun, Gunn	
MACMARTIN Cameron	
MACMASTER Buchanan, MacInnes	
MACMATH Matheson	
MACMAURICE Buchanan	
MACMENZIES Menzies	
MACMICHAEL Stewart	
MACMINN Menzies	
MACMONIES Menzies	
MACMORRAN Mackinnon	
MACMUNN Stewart	
MACMURCHIE, MACMURCHY Buchanan, MacDonald, Mackenzie	
MACMURDO MacDonald, Macpherson	
MACMURDOCH MacDonald, Macpherson	
MACMURRAY Murray	

MACMURRICH MacDonald, Macpherson	
MACMUTRIE Stewart	
MACNAIR, MACNAYER MacFarlane, MacNaughton	
MACNEE MacGregor	
MACNEILLY MacNeil	
MACNEISH MacGregor	
MACNEUR MacFarlane	
MACNIDER MacFarlane	
MACNIE MacGregor	
MACNISH MacGregor	
MACNITER MacFarlane	
MACNIVEN Cumming, Mackintosh, MacNaughton	
MACNUIR MacNaughton	
MACNUYER Buchanan, MacFarlane, MacNaughton	
MACONIE Cameron	
MACOUL, MACOWL MacDougall	
MACOWEN Campbell	
MACPATRICK Lamont, MacLaren	
MACPETER MacGregor	
MACPHATER MacLaren	
MACPHEDRAN Campbell, Macaulay	
MACPHEE, MACPHIE MacFie	
MACPHUN Campbell, Matheson	
MACQUAIRE MacQuarrie	
MACQUEY MacKay	
MACQUIHIRR MacQuarrie	
MACQUOID MacKay	
MACRA MacRae	
MACRAILD MacLeod	
MACRAITH MacDonald, MacRae	
MACRANKIN MacLean of Duart	
MACRATH MacRae	
MACRITCHIE Mackintosh	
MACROB, MACROBB Gunn, Innes, MacFarlane, Robertson	
MACROBBIE Drummond, Robertson	
MACROBERT Drummond, Robertson	
MACRORIE, MACRORY MacDonald	
MACRUER MacDonald	
MACRURIE, MACRURY MacDonald	

MACSHIMMIE	Fraser
MACSIMON	Fraser
MACSORLEY	Cameron, Lamont, MacDonald
MACSPORRAN	MacDonald
MACSUAIN	MacQueen
MACSWAN	MacDonald, MacQueen
MACSWEEN	MacQueen
MACSYMON	Fraser
MACTAUSE	Campbell
MACTEAR	MacIntyre, Ross
MACTIER, MACTIRE	Ross
MACURE	Campbell, MacIver
MACVAIL	Cameron, MacKay, Mackintosh, Macpherson
MACVANISH	Mackenzie
MACVARISH	MacDonald
MACVEAGH	MacDonald, MacLean of Duart
MACVICAR	Campbell, MacNaughton
MACVINISH	Mackenzie
MACVURIE	MacDonald
MACVURRICH	MacDonald, Macpherson
MACWALTER	MacFarlane
MACWATTIE	Buchanan
MACWHANNELL	MacDonald
MACWHIRR	MacQuarrie
MALCOLMSON	MacCallum, MacLeod, Malcolm
MALLOCH	MacGregor
MANN	Gunn
MANSON	Gunn
MARJORIBANKS	Johnstone
MARSHALL	Keith
MARTIN	Cameron, MacDonald
MASSEY	Matheson
MASTERTON	Buchanan
MATHIE	Matheson
MAY	MacDonald
MEANS	Menzies
MEIN, MEINE	Menzies
MELVIN	MacBeth
MENGUES	Menzies
MENNIE	Menzies

MENTEITH	Graham, Stewart
MEYNERS	Menzies
MICHIE	Forbes
MILLER	MacFarlane
MILNE	Gordon, Innes, Ogilvie
MINN	Menzies
MINNUS	Menzies
MITCHELL	Innes
MOIR	Gordon
MONACH	MacFarlane
MONTEITH	Graham, Stewart
MONZIE	Menzies
MORAY	Murray
MORE	Leslie
MORGAN	MacKay
MORRIS	Buchanan
MUNN	Stewart
MURCHIE	Buchanan
MURCHISON	Buchanan
MURDOCH	MacDonald, Macpherson
MURDOSON	MacDonald, Macpherson
NEIL, NEILL	MacNeil
NEILSON	MacKay, MacNeil
NEISH	MacGregor
NELSON	Gunn
NICOL, NICOLL	MacNicol
NISH	MacGregor
NIVEN	Cumming, Mackintosh
NOBLE	Mackintosh
OLIVER	Fraser
PARLANE	MacFarlane
PATERSON	Farquharson, MacLaren
PATRICK	Lamont
PAUL	Cameron, Mackintosh
PEARSON	Macpherson
PETER	MacGregor
PHILIPSON	MacDonell
PITULLICH	MacDonald
POLLARD	MacKay
POLSON	MacKay
PURCELL	MacDonald
REID	Murray, Robertson
REOCH	Farquharson, MacDonald

REVIE	MacDonald
RIACH	Farquharson, MacDonald
RICHARDSON	Ogilvie, Buchanan
RISK	Buchanan
RITCHIE	Mackintosh
ROBB	MacFarlane
ROBINSON	Gunn
ROBSON	Gunn
RONALD	MacDonell
RONALDSON	MacDonell
RORISON	MacDonald
ROY	Robertson
RUSKIN	Buchanan
SANDERSON	MacDonell
SANDISON	Gunn
SAUNDERS	MacAlister
SCOBIE	MacKay
SHANNON	MacDonald
SIM, SIME	Fraser
SIMON	Fraser
SIMPSON	Fraser
SKINNER	MacGregor
SMALL	Murray
SMART	Mackenzie
SORLEY	Cameron, Lamont, MacDonald
SPENCE	MacDuff
SPORRAN	MacDonald
STALKER	MacFarlane
STARK	Robertson
STRINGER	MacGregor
SUMMERS	Lindsay
SWAN	MacQueen
SWANSON	Gunn
SYME	Fraser
SYMON	Fraser
TAGGART	Ross
TARRILL	Mackintosh
TAWESSON	Campbell
TAWSE	Farquharson
THOMASON	Campbell
THOMPSON	Campbell, MacTavish
TOLMIE	MacLeod
TOSH	Mackintosh
TOSHACH	Mackintosh

TOWARD, TOWART	Lamont
TURNER	Lamont
TWEEDIE	Fraser
TYRE	MacIntyre
URE	Campbell
VASS	Munro, Ross
WALLIS	Wallace
WALTERS	Forbes
WASS	Munro, Ross
WATSON	Buchanan
WATT	Buchanan
WEAVER	MacFarlane
WHANNELL	MacDonald
WHITE, WHYTE	Lamont, MacGregor
WILKINSON	MacDonald
WILL	Gunn
WILLIAMSON	Gunn, MacKay
WRIGHT	MacIntyre
WYLIE	Gunn, MacFarlane
YUILL, YUILLE, YULE	Buchanan

Clan Societies

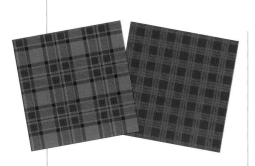

The Armstrong Clan
267 Roxton Drive
Waterloo
Ont. N2T 1R2

Clan Bell, Inc.
PO Box 451
Springfield
VT 05156, USA

**Blair Society For Genealogical
Research**
20W. College Avenue
Brownsburg
IN 46112-1253, USA

**Family of Bruce Society in
America**
19 Chestnut Street, Bristol
NH 03222, USA

Clan Buchan Association
2845 Lavender Lane
Green Bay
WI 54313, USA

Clan Campbell Society, NA
6412 Newcastle Road
Fayetteville
NC 28303-2137, USA

Clan Carmichael International
Clan Office
Carmichael
By Biggar
South Lanarkshire
ML12 6PG, Scotland

Clan Chisolm Society
1122 Highview Place
Sidney
BC V8L 5J9

Clan Davidson Society (USA)
7004 Barberry Drive
North Little Rock
AR 72118, USA

Clan Donald Canada
216 Cornell Drive
Port Stanley
Ont. N5L 1A5

Clan Dunbar
224 Riverview Road
Townsend
TN 37882, USA

Clan Ewen Society
PO Box 3
St. Peters
NS B0E 3B0

**Clan Farquharson Association
of Canada**
S.C.R. R.P.O.
PO Box 23045
Dartmouth
NS B3A 4S9

Clan Forsyth Society of Canada
342 Swinburne Road
Burlington
Ont. L7N 2A1

Clan Fraser Society of Canada
71 Charles Street E., Suite 1101
Toronto
Ont. M4Y 2TS

House of Gordon (Canada)
10 Elmer Avenue
Petawawa
Ont. K8H 2M2

Clan Graham Society
1228 Kensington Drive
High Point
NC 27262, USA

Clan Grant Society of Canada
6919 9th Line
Beeton
Ont. L0G 1A0

The Clan Gregor Society
Administrative Office
Mo Dhachaidh
2 Braehead
Alloa, Clacks
FK10 2EW, Scotland

Clan Gregor Society
316 Bedford Highway
Halifax
NS B3M 2K8

Clan Guthrie, USA, Inc.
PO Box 2981
Pittsfield
MA 01202, USA

Clan Hunter in Canada
61 Downing Crescent
London
Ont. N6A 3C7

Clan Irwin Association
226 1750th Avenue
Mt. Pulaski
IL 62548, USA

Jardine Clan Society
Heritage Garden West
305-1 Heritage Way
Lindsay
Ont. K9V 5P9

**The Clan MacBean Society
of Nova Scotia**
103 Chappell Street
Dartmouth
NS B3A 3P9

Clan MacCord Society
625 Hurd Avenue
Burlington
Ont. L75 1T4

**Clan Mackenzie Society in
the Americas**
Canadian Chapter
580 Rebecca Street
Oakville
Ont. L6K 3N9

**Clan MacKenzie Society of
Nova Scotia**
Merigonish
NS B0K 1G0

Clan Mackintosh of NA
46 Dunvegan Drive
Chatham
Ont. N7M 4Z8

Clan MacLean Association
231 Kemano Road
Aurora
Ont. L4G 4Z1

Clan MacMillan Society in NA
37 McDonald Street
St. Catherines
Ont. L2S 2M3

Clan MacNab Society of NA
8610 Lurline Avenue
Canoga Park
CA 91306, USA

Clan MacRae Society NA
306 Surrey Road
Savannah
GA 31410, USA

The Marjoribanks Family
2228 Kipling Street
Ottawa
Ont. K1H 6T5

Clan Matheson Society
30 Robert Allen Drive
Halifax
NS B3M 3G8

Clan Maxwell Society of Canada
111 Bruce Street, Suite 416
Kirkland
Que. H9H 4B7

Clan Maxwell Society of Canada
282 Shamrock Court
Oshawa
Ont. L1J 6X9

Clan Menzies Society of Canada
Rowan's End
751 Spragge Crescent
Cobourg
Ont. K9A 2T6

Mowat Family International
Box 1334
162 Main Street West
Stouffville
Ont. L4A 8A3

Clan Napier in NA
3886 West 36th Avenue
Vancouver
BC V6N 256

Clan Pollock
12712 St Clair Drive
Middletown
KY 40243-1037, USA

Clan Rattray Society
RR1, Walsingham
Ont. N0E 1X0

Clan Maxwell Society of Canada
282 Shamrock Court
Oshawa
Ont. L1J 6X9

**Clan Ross Association of
Canada, Inc.**
66 Crestwood Crescent
Winnipeg
Man. R2J 1H6

Clan Scott Society
PO Box 13021, Austin
TX 78711-3021, USA

**Clan Sinclair Association
Inc. (USA)**
133 Major Street
Toronto
Ont. M5S 2KQ

**Clan Stewart Society in
America, Inc.**
Box 85, R.R. 1
Little Britain
Ont. K0M 2C0

Clan Urquhart Association
North American Branch
56 Waldorf Drive, Akron
OH 44313, USA

Index

Acknowledgements

As always, I am indebted to Ian Chilvers for the use of his extensive library and his encyclopaedic memory. Mike Sherborne offered moral support and Maggie Ramsay provided useful reference material. I would also like to thank Diane Dewar, Ann Farquhar, Lesley Lonie, Ross and Margaret Millar, Daphne Miller, Helen Mowat, and Elizabeth Peart for their insights into Scottish life.

Collins and Brown would like to thank the Scottish Tartans Society not only for supplying the tartans but for being on hand to help with numerous other queries.

Thanks also to Malcolm Innes for lending Collins and Brown the kilt and Highland dress featured on pages 10–12.

All of the tartans and the three McIan prints on pages 13 and 129 were supplied by the Scottish Tartans Society, Port-na-Craig Road, Pitlochry, Perthshire PH16 5ND.

Heraldic crests were illustrated by Romilly Squire, Heraldic Artist at the Court of the Lord Lyon and Deputy Secretary of the Standing Council of Scottish Chiefs.

PICTURE CREDITS

All of the photographs in this book are the copyright of Sam Lloyd, except those listed below.

Front and back cover David Lyons; Page 24 left Private Scottish Collection; page 25 top left Crown Copyright: reproduced by Permission of Historic Scotland; page 28 top right Dennis Hardley Photography; page 29 centre (Trustees of the National Museums of Scotland; page 29 bottom right The Scottish Highland Photo Library; page 33 centre The Scottish National Portrait Gallery; page 42 David Lyons; page 43 bottom right David Lyons; page 53 bottom right Dennis Hardley Photography; page 62 David Lyons; page 66 David Lyons; page 76 top right The Scottish National Portrait Gallery; page 79 top right (Trustees of the National Museums of Scotland; page 92 top right David Lyons; page 116 top right The Scottish National Portrait Gallery; page 120 bottom left The Scottish National Portrait Gallery; page 124 left The Scottish National Portrait Gallery; page 125 bottom right David Lyons; page 126 top right The Scottish National Portrait Gallery; page 129 right David Lyons.

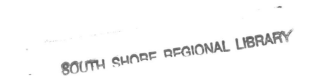